RAPTORS *of the* WEST
Captured in Photographs

KATE DAVIS

Photographs by Rob Palmer, Nick Dunlop, and Kate Davis

Mountain Press Publishing Company
Missoula, Montana
2011

D1441737

Library of Congress Cataloging-in-Publication Data

Davis, Kate, 1959-
  Raptors of the West : captured in photographs / Kate Davis ; photographs by Rob Palmer,
Nick Dunlop, and Kate Davis.
      p. cm.
  Includes bibliographical references and index.
  ISBN 978-0-87842-575-4 (pbk. : alk. paper)
  1. Birds of prey—West (U.S.) 2. Birds of prey—West (U.S.)—Pictorial works. I. Palmer, Rob
(Robert Michael), 1953-. II. Dunlop, Nick. III. Title.
  QL677.78.D384 2011
  598.90978--dc22

                              2011010002

                       PRINTED IN HONG KONG

MP Mountain Press
PUBLISHING COMPANY
P.O. Box 2399 • Missoula, MT 59806 • 406-728-1900
800-234-5308 • info@mtnpress.com
www.mountain-press.com

Contents

Preface

For some of us, birds of prey are much more than a chance encounter in the out-of-doors; raptors are our lives. Rob, Nick, and I have a myriad of interests but would agree that what fuels the fire and keeps us going are birds of prey. The three of us met at the Raptor Research Foundation Conference in Bakersfield, California, in 2004. This one was a joint gathering with the California Hawking Club. Falconers were everywhere, and each registrant was asked at the front desk of the motel if they would be checking in with a bird.

Rob and Nick were selling their images, huge panels of photographs facing each other at the entryway. This was the first time they'd met, and a mutual admiration and friendship developed right there in the showroom. This was my first conference and I was to present research that Christopher Templeton, Erick Greene, and I had done, "Allometry of alarm calls: Black-capped chickadees encode information about predator size in their mobbing calls." Little did I know that my life would change right then and there with all of those fellow raptorphiles under one roof.

I approached Rob about collaborating on a book called *Falcons of North America*, which was still in the proposal stage, and he got Nick to jump on the bandwagon. It would be four years and a thousand emails and phone calls before we had the book in our hands. It came out just in time for the 2008 Raptor Research Foundation Conference, which my organization, Raptors of the Rockies, hosted here in Missoula, Montana. The three of us flipped through the book for the first time together, surrounded by raptor biologists from around the world.

Both photographers had sent hundreds of images for the falcon book, which resulted in an often-difficult selection process. When the dust settled and great feedback began coming in on the text and images, we decided to showcase more photos with *Raptors of the West*. We had a meeting at Nick's house in the Bay Area the following April. We had intended to spend several days going through the photographs that we already had and making a shopping list of those we still needed to get. This was a business trip of sorts, with the best of intentions. Instead, we spent our days on a whirlwind photography spree. Up early to check out coastal marshes and cliffs, we shot hunting Peregrines, nesting Great Horned Owls, and an egret rookery in a downtown condo development—all favorite haunts of Nick's. When our subject was spotted taking flight or doing something else interesting, the burst of camera shutters between the three of us was deafening. We might not have gotten a lot done on the book, but we promised to make this an annual event.

When it came to the format for *Raptors of the West*, I decided that an interesting presentation of the forty-five species would be by the habitats and regions in which they *breed*. Arguments will be made about my grouping, and rightly so, but we wanted a different scheme than the scores of bird books that present species in taxonomic order, or classification of who is related to whom. Instead we decided to feature our birds by who lives near whom: hawks and falcons, eagles and owls, vultures and Ospreys, mixed together in the many landscapes they inhabit. We hope to have some surprises as our readers peruse raptors from the Arctic tundra to the desert Southwest, falcons to owls—supreme predators all.

Acknowledgments

To round out the book we enlisted the expertise of friends who provided wonderful photographs of species we were seeking, and we appreciate their help.

THANKS TO
Gerald Romanchuk • BT "Tad" Lubinski • Jeff Wohl • Miguel Lasa • Erick Greene • David Palmer

We are elated to have two expert reviewers on board. Grainger Hunt, senior scientist at the Peregrine Fund, wrote his master's thesis on the Padre Peregrines in 1966. He has since studied eagles, falcons, and the California Condor, with over fifty publications and reports, several with wife, Terry, who is also a biologist.

Hans Peeters has been a leading artist and author in the raptor world for decades, and a friend since we met at the Woodson Birds in Art exhibition in 1993, and again at the 2004 Bakersfield Raptor Research Foundation/California Hawking Club Conference. His books, including *Raptors of California* and *Field Guide to Owls of California and the West*, are the best out there, and his paintings are superlative. Hans helped with the owl species.

Special thanks to my best friend and lover of all wild creatures, Sally Phillips, my mom. —KD

Northern Goshawk. —KATE DAVIS

Introduction

Known as top predators, expert hunters, icons of the bird world, and birds of prey, raptors are like nothing else on earth. They comprise the order Falconiformes (hawks, falcons, eagles, Osprey, secretary birds, and New World vultures) and order Strigiformes (owls). These are two groups of unrelated birds that have one thing in common: a predatory way of life.

I have noticed that another word is constantly applied when discussing raptors, either as a compliment or a mistake: *rapture*, as in headlines for newspaper and magazine articles, "The Rapture of Flight," "Raptor Raptures," or "Enraptured with Raptors." I have been running an educational program called Raptors of the Rockies for the last twenty-three years (another headline: "Enraptured in the Rockies") and have given a couple thousand programs and tours. Locally, not a month passes that someone doesn't ask me, "Aren't you the rapture woman?" Of the two options mentioned, I consider that to be a compliment.

Perhaps it isn't a coincidence that people associate raptors with rapture. Chances are they don't realize that *raptor* and *rapture* both come from the same Latin word, *rapere*, which means "to seize" or "to carry away." But they do know there is something special about raptors. In the Biblical concept of the Rapture, Christ will be reborn. The association of raptors with religion dates back thousands of years, with depictions of raptors as deities and gods. In ancient Egypt, Horus the Falcon was god of the sky, goddesses were represented by Griffon Vultures, and a bird known as Ba frequented ancient tombs.

On this continent, the story of the Thunderbird—a huge, all-powerful raptor that personifies thunder, lightning, and even rainfall—is widespread among indigenous people. In the Far North, belief is that the Thunderbird created the world. Native peoples also consider eagle feathers to be sacred. Religions and cultures around the world have revered raptors, continuing to this day. They represent stealth, strength, and success, qualities that may be sought after and envied by mortals.

The other meaning of the word *rapture* involves wild enthusiasm and ecstasy, emotions that certainly come to the surface when watching raptors: their aerial prowess and the thrill of the hunt rival any spectacle in the animal world. Even the casual observer might find it hard not to cheer for an Osprey's headfirst dive at a fish or a 200 mph stoop (steep dive) by a falcon. We may never forget being startled by the silent flight of a nocturnal owl, or transfixed by their resonant calls. The seemingly effortless mastery of the sky by a vulture, eagle, or hawk playing in thermals is a sight that can be etched in our minds. With their incredible beauty, fierce beaks and talons, and impressive plumage, their eyes suggesting an attitude of steely determination, raptors are worthy of deep respect. Perhaps without realizing it, we are all *Enraptured with Raptors*.

Arctic Tundra and Boreal Forests

A subspecies of the Red-tailed Hawk, the Harlan's Hawk summers in Alaska and northern British Columbia, spending winters across much of the western United States.
—KATE DAVIS

Mystery and romance encompass the domain of the Far North. How can animals make a living, or even survive, in such a formidable climate? With its glorious landscapes and the rich breeding grounds of the tundra in summer, the Land of the Midnight Sun is appealing, but the long, dark, frigid winters demand a certain respect. Apart from the occasional resilient occupant of Canada or Alaska, few bird enthusiasts venture into the Arctic, so most people only know it from film, television, and photographs.

Encircling the North Pole and extending south to the taiga, the treeless Arctic tundra has a permanently frozen layer of soil, or permafrost. Life on the Arctic tundra is limited by cold temperatures, low precipitation, poor soils, and high winds. The average winter temperature in some areas is minus 30 degrees Fahrenheit. Most animals breed during the summer growing season, which lasts around fifty to sixty days and has an average temperature between 37 and 54 degrees Fahrenheit.

The boreal forest, or taiga, lies just south of the tundra. It is made up of coniferous forests—sparse and scraggly where they meet the tundra, and thicker and lusher toward the south and near the coasts. Even though it is the largest land biome, or habitat type, in the world, the diversity of plant and animal species is low. The seasons are basically just a short summer and

long winter, so it's either warm and humid or extremely cold, with average high temperatures of about 70 degrees Fahrenheit in summer and well below zero most of the winter. Some raptors tough it out, but many more fly further south for several months each year.

The largest and perhaps most impressive among falcons, a Gyrfalcon flying the cliffs in the months of darkness is a haunting sight. The powerful flight of the huge Snowy Owl isn't very owl-like; it happens in daylight, and is more reminiscent of a hawk or even a giant falcon. The entire population of Arctic breeding Rough-legged Hawks passes through taiga country and winters in open treeless habitats farther south, scattered across the landscape for five months a year.

The nocturnal Boreal Owl is very adept at flying through dense vegetation, zigging and zagging and not touching a leaf. Quite the opposite, the Northern Hawk Owl loves to perch in the bright sun, often at the top of a snag or tree from where it launches quick, low flights to secure prey. The Great Gray Owl is the largest North American owl in overall length (but not mass—that's the Snowy) and is similarly easy to spot during the day, often quite approachable by humans. The raptors of the Far North don't make it onto many birders' life lists, but when they do, it's an unforgettable experience.

Snowy Owl

The heaviest owl in North America, the huge and unmistakable Snowy Owl inhabits treeless Arctic tundra around the Northern Hemisphere. Although it was once in its own genus, *Nyctea*, recent genetic studies have determined that it belongs in the genus *Bubo*, along with the Great Horned Owl. —NICK DUNLOP

Snowy Owls are nomadic, their movements largely dictated by fluctuating lemming populations. When lemming populations crash an irruption may occur, with huge numbers of Snowy Owls venturing south to winter in the United States. Probably the record irruption was during the winter of 1927–28, when well over two thousand Snowy Owls were counted in a dozen states, and about half that number ended up in taxidermy shops in Canada. —ROB PALMER

Snowy Owls are patient hunters, waiting on a low perch, hilltop, rocky outcrop, or building for long periods, hoping to detect movement. Females are more heavily marked, like this first-year bird. —ROB PALMER

The dense, downy plumage of a Snowy Owl is adapted to provide exceptional insulation against frigid Arctic temperatures. Like most owls, they have fine feathers covering their legs. In addition the beak is mostly tucked away in feathers on the face. Snowy Owl feathers lack the sound-reducing structures found in the plumage of nocturnal woodland owls.
—ROB PALMER

Adult males are entirely white, or nearly so. Females and juveniles are barred with dark brown or black. Primarily visual hunters, they also have acute hearing and can detect prey under a blanket of snow. —ROB PALMER

Because they spend much of their lives in the remote Arctic, Snowy Owls tend to be unafraid of people, sometimes moving right into civilization and creating a stir for birders and raptor neophytes alike. —ROB PALMER

In peak years, Snowy Owls might eat nothing but lemmings—sometimes as many as five a day. When food is abundant, females can lay up to eleven eggs with a breeding territory as small as a half-mile square. They do not breed at all in years when lemming populations crash. —ROB PALMER

Along with lemmings, voles, and other small rodents, Snowy Owls may take large game like rabbits, as well as other birds. Hans Peeters says that in pursuit of birds in the air, "the flight of this owl suggests that of an enormous falcon." —ROB PALMER

The largest falcon in the world, the Gyrfalcon is an Arctic specialist. Flashing across the eye of this young female is the transparent third eyelid, or nictitating membrane, which protects, moistens, and cleans the eye.
—ROB PALMER

Researchers that analyzed feather and fecal samples at an active Gyrfalcon nest in Greenland found that it had been used more or less continuously for 2,500 years, the most extreme long-term nest use of any raptor ever documented.
—NICK DUNLOP

Gyrfalcons have long been used in the sport of falconry. In the Middle Ages, social rank determined which raptor species a person could keep, with white Gyrfalcons reserved for the king with the most clout. —ROB PALMER

Gyrfalcons have been spared many of the human-caused hazards that have tormented other raptors. Their isolation in the undeveloped north has left them largely unmolested by humans and free of contaminants like pesticides. —ROB PALMER

Although Gyrfalcons can take birds such as ptarmigans in the air, they usually catch prey on the ground, even forcing birds to land before pouncing. Mammals like ground squirrels are favorite prey, especially in the spring. Coastal Gyrfalcons take more seabirds and waterfowl than inland Gyrfalcons do. —ROB PALMER

Female and immature Gyrfalcons are more likely to migrate to the continental United States in autumn. Males often remain on the breeding grounds over the long, frigid winter, hunting in the 24-hour-a-day darkness. —ROB PALMER

Gyrfalcons are monotypic, meaning there is only one species, but very polymorphic, meaning individual birds occur in a wide array of color morphs, also known as variants. Gray is the most common color morph in North America, with geographic trends between light, gray, and dark. However, different color morphs may also live side by side. —KATE DAVIS

A trained Gyrfalcon belonging to Tom Cade was the subject of a famous 1998 study of falcon flight speeds. The bird, Kumpan, was clocked diving at speeds of over 200 kilometers per hour, or about 130 mph. —NICK DUNLOP

Cliff nesters, Gyrfalcons often take over the stick nests of other raptors and ravens. Ledge nests like this one in Alaska usually have an overhang to keep off the snow and rain. —ROB PALMER

A young Gyrfalcon catches her breath after killing a hen pheasant. —NICK DUNLOP

Northern Hawk Owl

With its small eyes and facial disc, fast noisy flight, and pointy wings, as well as the fact that it hunts by sight during the day, the aptly named Northern Hawk Owl may seem to have more in common with hawks and falcons than with other owls. This is a young bird, as indicated by its dark mask and short tail. —GERALD ROMANCHUK

Like so many of the Arctic and boreal forest species that rarely see people, Northern Hawk Owls are approachable, making them great subjects for photographers. —ROB PALMER

A Northern Hawk Owl nest was found on the Rocky Mountain Front in Montana in 2010, representing perhaps the most southerly breeders of this species. This breeding pair inhabited a lodgepole forest that had burned three years earlier. Here the male has made a prey delivery. —JEFF WOHL

The hunting strategy of Northern Hawk Owls has been described as shrike-like. Using a tall vantage point to scan for rodents, an owl will swoop in quickly, dipping low to grab the prey and swooping up to another tall perch. The photographer has baited this bird with a mouse. —ROB PALMER

Like many northern raptor species, Northern Hawk Owls are nomadic, following fluctuating vole populations. —ROB PALMER

With their dark gray plumage, fledgling Northern Hawk Owls differ from adults in appearance—so much so that at one point birdwatchers in Europe even thought they had found a new species, described as resembling a Spectacled Owl of South America. —JEFF WOHL

Like most owl fledglings, young Northern Hawk Owls stick together. They are often found near the nest for six to eight weeks after fledging. —JEFF WOHL

The irises of Rough-legged Hawks change from light brown, gray, or yellow to dark brown as they mature. To cool off, a Rough-legged Hawk pants and rapidly vibrates its throat—an action known as gular fluttering. —KATE DAVIS

Called a Rough-legged Buzzard in the Old World, the common and scientific names describe the feathered tarsi, or legs: *Buteo lagopus* means "hare-footed hawk." —ROB PALMER

Rough-legged Hawks migrate at low altitudes and have been known to roost communally in winter; one winter roost in Montana contained 250 individuals. Research suggests that these act as "information centers," allowing hawks to find food locally by following successful hunters. —ROB PALMER

All summer Rough-legged Hawks catch mostly lemmings and voles, switching to voles and mice on the southern winter hunting grounds. Their tiny beaks and feet are extremely effective weapons for attacking these small mammals. —KATE DAVIS

Unlike other buteos, such as Red-tailed Hawks, with which they share their wintering grounds, Rough-legs often perch on tiny limbs and little twigs, perches that look impossibly delicate for such big birds. —KATE DAVIS

Rough-legged Hawks are more aerial in their hunting than most other buteos. They are often seen coursing or remaining motionless over a particularly inviting bit of ground, either hovering (with wings beating) or kiting (with wings spread motionless) in the wind as they watch for prey. —ROB PALMER

Almost the entire population of Rough-legs leaves the Arctic breeding grounds in late August and September, flies south past the boreal forest, and spends the winter in southernmost Canada and most of the Lower 48, females remaining farther north than males. —KATE DAVIS

Sexes are fairly close in length, but females are heavier. Males, such as this one, have several bars on the tail; females have one terminal tail band.
—ROB PALMER

Rough-legged Hawks spend the winter in open-country prairies, marshes, and grasslands—areas similar to their summer home in the Arctic tundra. —ROB PALMER

This bird's dark bellyband and carpal patch (the patch at the bend of the wing) are characteristic of juvenile and adult female Rough-legged Hawks. Their steady, efficient wing beats are unhurried and graceful. —ROB PALMER

Great Gray Owl

The Great Gray Owl is a huge raptor, the largest owl in North America in overall length. With a small body covered in dense, soft, insulating feathers it is not the heaviest, however. That distinction belongs to Great Horned and Snowy Owls. The small yellow eyes of this diurnal hunter are surrounded by concentric rings like a bull's-eye. —BT "TAD" LUBINSKI

Great Gray Owls may skip several years between nests in times of low rodent abundance. Stick Goshawk nests are often usurped; in this case a broken off stump held two babies. The young begin to leave the nest at about 20 to 29 days old, unable to fly yet but hopping, flapping, and climbing in the surrounding trees. —BT "TAD" LUBINSKI

A Great Gray Owl stretches a foot and wing. Although Great Grays are quite approachable by people most of the year, a female with chicks can turn into an aggressive terror that will strike anyone who ventures too close to her nest. —BT "TAD" LUBINSKI

The preferred hunting tactic of the Great Gray Owl is to locate prey from a post, bush or tree, often appearing mesmerized by movements or sounds below. After a silent glide in, the owl secures and swallows its meal, usually a rodent, whole in seconds. —BT "TAD" LUBINSKI

Pinpointing the exact location of its prey, a Great Gray Owl hovers over the snow. —BT "TAD" LUBINSKI

Great Gray Owls have a large, round facial disc, which helps direct sound to the hidden, asymmetrical ear openings on either side of the head. While perched, they also bob their heads up and down and turn them from side to side, presumably to help judge distance by viewing an object from different angles. —BT "TAD" LUBINSKI

Even though it is such a big predator, the Great Gray Owl mainly just feeds on small rodents, especially voles and pocket gophers. If prey numbers crash, Great Grays often move in a "starvation migration" rather than switch to a diet of larger mammals or birds. —BT "TAD" LUBINSKI

Great Gray Owls have the remarkable skill of punching through snow up to a foot and a half deep to retrieve rodents burrowing below, often plunging headfirst. This attests to their extraordinary hearing and strength—and to their patience. —BT "TAD" LUBINSKI

Boreal Owl

Boreal Owls are largely nocturnal, hunting from low perches and switching locations every several minutes, listening for prey scurrying under snow and debris.
—GERALD ROMANCHUK

Boreal and Saw-whet Owls have the most asymmetrical ears of all owls. The left ear opening is located low on the head and faces downward, whereas the right ear opening is higher and faces upward. This arrangement allows Boreal Owls to detect prey with incredible precision. —GERALD ROMANCHUK

Young birds like these look nothing like their parents. Young give peeping calls to be fed. Male Boreal Owls may call for hours, with their "song" audible over a mile away, and one estimate of 4,000 hoots in a night. —GERALD ROMANCHUK

The Boreal Owl is like a larger, northern-coniferous-forest version of the Saw-whet Owl, its face framed by black bars and white eyebrows. Secretive and nocturnal, breeding pairs were only fairly recently discovered in several states and Ontario. —GERALD ROMANCHUK

Like most raptors, Boreal Owls exhibit reverse sexual size dimorphism, meaning females are larger than males. Female Boreal Owls weigh as much as 43 percent more than males and tend to eat larger voles and fewer birds than the smaller, more agile males.
—GERALD ROMANCHUK

Fields, Grasslands, and Prairies

A Peregrine Falcon on the Rocky Mountain Front of Montana. —KATE DAVIS

With their vast, open landscapes—often punctuated by twisting rivers and streams, abrupt bluffs, and mountain ranges—grasslands and prairies hold a surprising diversity of plant and animal life. In the American West most of these grasslands, including the Great Plains and California's Central Valley, occur in semiarid areas with moderate rainfall and hot summers. Many grasslands have fertile soil and have been converted to agricultural use, monocultures that offer scanty food supplies, resulting in larger home ranges for raptor inhabitants.

As the ground heats by midmorning, raptors riding thermals often dot the immense sky that stretches from horizon to horizon. Long-range foraging hunts by Golden Eagles may cover tens of miles, with a parent returning to the cliff eyrie with a rabbit or squirrel for the chicks. A Ferruginous Hawk pair may need just a slight rise in terrain for nesting, or their bulky bundle of selected sticks in a solitary tree may be seen for miles. Great numbers of Swainson's Hawks congregate in the fall, changing their diet from rodents to the near-plague of grasshoppers before their long southerly migration. Dramatic weather changes roll across the countryside, bringing black sheets of rain that cause Burrowing Owls families to dive for cover underground, returning to the surface for a sunbath after the storm has subsided.

The colorful little falcon hovering in place like a hummingbird in slow motion is the American Kestrel, scanning the immediate area below for an unlucky rodent tunneling through the grass. The larger version darting out from a dirt embankment, pothole, or cliff face is the Prairie Falcon, cryptic coloration hiding the youngsters until they appear screaming and scrambling when their parents arrive with a food delivery.

While the sweeping vistas may allow us to spot raptors at a great distance, they may also put us at a disadvantage since the bird may perceive us as a threat and flee. Often, a chance encounter may last only a few seconds, but if we are lucky, we may be treated to the spectacle of a courtship flight or hunting foray. The fields, grasslands, and prairies offer it all in an oversized and impressive show.

Swainson's Hawks, like many of the buteos, or soaring hawks, have several color morphs. This exceptionally dark six-month-old female is one example. Today, as an adult, she is nearly all black with white lores (the area between the eyes and beak). —KATE DAVIS

An adult in flight. Note the characteristic dark flight feathers with lighter wing coverts. Nearly all Swainson's Hawks migrate from temperate North America to Argentina, a distance of up to 6,200 miles one way! —ROB PALMER

Swainson's Hawks often hunt from an elevated spot like a utility pole or this isolated snag. They may also follow tractors tilling up soil or hunt the edges of grass fires to catch fleeing rodents. —NICK DUNLOP

Swainson's Hawks gang up in the fall, with flocks of young and old alike fattening up on grasshoppers in preparation for the long trek south. Some flocks can reach 10,000 birds, with over 800,000 passing over the geographic bottleneck of Veracruz, Mexico, in a season. —KATE DAVIS

A Swainson's Hawk swallows whole a huge snake, a favorite food item in regions where the reptiles are abundant. Elsewhere, these raptors hunt mostly rodents such as mice, voles, pocket gophers, and ground squirrels during the breeding season. Over the winter Swainson's Hawks almost exclusively eat insects: crickets, beetles, and as many as one hundred grasshoppers in one day. —ROB PALMER

A rufous morph Swainson's female awaits a food delivery by her mate. —NICK DUNLOP

With three main color morphs plus intermediate phases and juvenal plumages, perched Swainson's Hawks can be tricky to identify in the field. Dark morph birds are more often female and are more common farther west, especially in California. —KATE DAVIS

Swainson's Hawks mating, an activity that may be performed hundreds of times for one clutch of eggs. The male may be trying to ensure that it is indeed his progeny that he is raising since his mate is often left alone with nest duties while he is hunting. Many raptors copulate even when young are present in the nest, so it may also reinforce pair bonding. —ROB PALMER

Typical adult birds sport a dark "bib" between a light chin and belly. The Swainson's Hawk is truly a Raptor of the West, with most of the birds spending half the year on the prairies and grasslands of the intermountain United States. —NICK DUNLOP

The discovery in Argentina of thousands of wintering Swainson's Hawks killed by organophosphate insecticides in 1995 and 1996 led to the banning of the poison, and these hawks are now embraced by the local populace. —ROB PALMER

Burrowing Owl

Burrowing Owls are open-country grassland and prairie birds, colloquially called Ground Owls or Howdy Owls because of their habit of bowing as if in a greeting. Photographer Rob Palmer spent months with several owl families in the Pawnee National Grassland of Colorado. —ROB PALMER

The male Burrowing Owl has a lighter facial disc, is not as barred below, and may be somewhat "bleached out" after a summer in the sun compared to the female, who completes most of the incubation duties underground. She also has worn feathers on her sides from scrambling in and out of the burrow. —ROB PALMER

A mother and young at the nest entrance with a decoration that appears to be a shed snake skin. In what is unusual behavior compared to most owls, Burrowing Owls collect items, such as dried scraps of skin, bone, and cloth, to scatter around the burrow entrance and line the burrow and nest chamber. They are especially fond of cow and horse manure, which has been found to attract dung beetles, an important food source, especially for the youngsters. —ROB PALMER

These owls feed largely on insects that they catch in the air or pounce on from a hover. They also chase prey on foot. Most numerous are grasshoppers, beetles, and crickets, as well as "injurious" rodents that damage human crops, plus the occasional bird or reptile. —ROB PALMER

This young owl looks pumped up but is actually in a rouse—raising the feathers, shaking them, and laying them back down, an activity performed many times a day, especially after eating, a rain shower, or a dust bath. —ROB PALMER

What looks like an uncomfortable perch actually offers a vista to spot predators and prey. A few such elevated spots are essential to a successful nest site. Burrowing Owls historically nested in open grasslands, prairies, and deserts—usually near prairie dog towns. While still found in such places, they are becoming increasingly tolerant of humans, nesting at airports, golf courses, cemeteries, and vacant lots, and even in artificial nest burrows. —ROB PALMER

Burrowing Owl flight is briefer than that of the larger owls, with long undulations between wing beats. —ROB PALMER

In yet another of their endearing behaviors, Burrowing Owls commonly tilt their heads to one side like a curious puppy. Although the reason for this behavior is not certain, it probably helps them pinpoint the source of a sound. —ROB PALMER

Burrowing Owls may be semicolonial, with several families nesting together, especially at a prairie dog town. The rodents clip the grass low, making it easier for all to spot danger.
—ROB PALMER

With its long legs, short tail, and flattish head there's no mistaking a Burrowing Owl. Here a newly fledged young enjoys the last rays of daylight. Although commonly seen during the day, these birds can be active at any hour.
—ROB PALMER

Burrowing Owls can lay up to thirteen eggs in a clutch, but these seven babies with the mother are a more typical brood size. The young in the burrow are known to imitate the buzz of a rattlesnake, which may fool some potential predators—but probably not a real rattlesnake! —ROB PALMER

Despite their name Burrowing Owls rarely excavate their own burrows. These owls take over the burrows of mammals such as prairie dogs, ground squirrels, and marmots—even dens of potential predators like badgers, foxes, and skunks. Occasionally they commandeer a tortoise tunnel. —ROB PALMER

Northern populations of Burrowing Owls migrate to the southern Great Plains and Mexico in "leapfrog" fashion—Canadian birds leapfrog over those in the United States and winter farther south. —ROB PALMER

Taking a break in the heat, this owl intently watches an ant—too small to consider as a meal—go about its business. —ROB PALMER

Newly fledged siblings engage in a bout of play at the mouth of the burrow. Parents may bring injured prey items back to the nest so the young can practice their predation skills.
—ROB PALMER

Curiously, unlike Burrowing Owls elsewhere, Burrowing Owls in Florida and the Caribbean may make their own burrows in sandy soils where tunnels are absent. They dig with their beak and talons and kick backward with their feet.
—ROB PALMER

Play continues in a sort of King of the Hill contest. Burrowing Owls are among the most popular of species for both amateur and hard-core birdwatchers.
—ROB PALMER

Golden Eagle

Arguably one of the most magnificent Raptors of the West, the Golden Eagle is thought to be highly evolved, having perhaps the keenest eyesight of all animals. This species lives across the Northern Hemisphere in open country, preferably devoid of human activities. —KATE DAVIS

A Golden Eagle's age may be guessed by the degree of white at the base of the wing and tail feathers, with adult plumage attained at five years. This is a hatch-year bird, with all feathers the same age with minimal wear and a white "window" at the wrist. —KATE DAVIS

Golden Eagles prey upon a wide variety of species using tactics ranging from soaring and diving to low contour flights and sneak attacks. Although they typically eat rabbits and medium-sized rodents like marmots and prairie dogs, they will also take birds and mammals as large as deer and pronghorns. Ring-necked pheasants are regionally a secondary prey item, especially in the Great Plains. —ROB PALMER

The parents of this brood are excellent providers, with a cache of jackrabbit legs in the nest next to one unhatched egg. —NICK DUNLOP

A three- to four-week-old baby at the nest. The young fledge, fully feathered, at around eleven or twelve weeks of age. —ROB PALMER

Golden Eagles may have home ranges for nesting and foraging of up to 20 square miles. The extent of ranging depends on food supplies and may be relatively small in areas where prey is abundant. —NICK DUNLOP

Like most raptor species, Golden Eagles exhibit reverse sexual size dimorphism, with females larger than males, like this female on the right. —ROB PALMER

This eagle is delivering a load of hay, swiped from a pile left by a rancher to feed his cows, to add to the nest. —NICK DUNLOP

A solitary egg remains in a cliff nest in Colorado that offers a commanding view of the surrounding terrain but was abandoned for unknown reasons. Golden Eagles also build nests in trees, on the ground, and even on human-made structures like towers and platforms. —ROB PALMER

Golden Eagles belong to the genus *Aquila*, the true eagles. In 1937 Arthur Bent famously wrote that the Golden Eagle is "majestic in flight, regal in appearance, [and] dignified in manner. . . . Its hunting is like that of the noble falcons, clean, spirited, and dashing."
—ROB PALMER

Golden Eagles often disarticulate large prey for their young. Here a father brings in part of a young coyote pup. The male does nearly all of the hunting initially, with the female resuming hunting when the young are large enough to be left unattended and food demands increase. —NICK DUNLOP

Exercise on the nest involves a great deal of wing flapping, building muscles and coordination in preparation for fledging. Chicks are still fed by the parents for weeks or even months after fledging, after which they stray farther from the nest and begin to hunt on their own. —NICK DUNLOP

56

The female patiently presents morsels of food to the chicks. The young are able to feed themselves in the nest at about five weeks, ripping into carcasses on their own. —NICK DUNLOP

The Prairie Falcon is another true Raptor of the West, blending into the arid rocky and sandy surroundings. This is a male, called a tiercel for falcons. It comes from the Latin word *tertius*, meaning "third," perhaps because male falcons are roughly one-third smaller than females. —KATE DAVIS

The dark "armpits" on the underwings, known as axillaries, are a telltale field mark. —ROB PALMER

Perhaps the epitome of the wild and scenic West: a Prairie Falcon rides thermals over the Big Sandy River in Wyoming with snowcapped peaks as a backdrop. —ROB PALMER

In this sequence, a Prairie Falcon has an encounter with a raven, probably in play, but as falcons are mischievous he probably deserved being reprimanded with a feather pull. —ROB PALMER

Prairie Falcon nesting is timed to coincide with the presence of plentiful ground squirrels so the birds can have their pick of naive young animals at their peak. When some squirrel species estivate, retreating to their burrows for months on end to escape the heat, Prairie Falcons often head north and east to hunt another ground squirrel species that is still active.
—ROB PALMER

A Prairie Falcon's diet changes from ground squirrels all summer to birds in the winter, especially Western Meadowlarks and Horned Larks, usually caught on the ground or in low flight.
—ROB PALMER

A pair of Prairie Falcons has taken over the stick nest of a raven or hawk. Prairies tend to nest in potholes and cracks in the rock more than Peregrines, with whom they may share a cliff. Peregrines have been known to steal a squirrel or two from Prairie Falcons—a variation from their typical avian diet. —ROB PALMER

The white mutes (waste) on this ledge, used year after year, can be seen for nearly a mile. A third youngster—perhaps afraid of his larger sisters—climbed above the ledge and was fed separately 10 feet away. —ROB PALMER

Some Prairie Falcons engage in a three-tier loop migration, leaving the breeding grounds when the young fledge, spending the summer in another location, and wintering in a third location. Other populations stay put year-round. —NICK DUNLOP

Hunting tactics vary. They include launching from a perch or cliff; high soaring, or "prospecting"; and cruising fast and low over the terrain. —ROB PALMER

Because of their largely mammalian diet, Prairie Falcons fared better in the days of widespread use of the pesticide DDT after World War II. In contrast, Peregrines, which feed on birds, were nearly wiped out in North America due to the effects of biomagnification (the increasing concentration of toxins in animals' bodies higher up the food chain). —KATE DAVIS

The Prairie Falcon is about the same size as the Peregrine and may be confused with young Peregrines, whose plumage is similar. Prairie Falcons have a white superciliary line, or eyebrow, white cheeks and throat, and a thin malar stripe, or mustache. —ROB PALMER

63

The Snake River Birds of Prey National Conservation Area in Idaho boasts the highest densities of breeding raptors in the world. Prairie Falcons have nested on virtually every available rock face, occasionally two on a cliff, stacked vertically. —NICK DUNLOP

Pairs establish their breeding territory early in the season and defend it in patrols of the boundaries. Attacks are especially vigorous when the young hatch, decreasing as they get older. At feeding time a seemingly vacant cliff will come alive, cryptically colored babies flapping and cackling at adults. —ROB PALMER

Prairie Falcons live far from people in a harsh environment that, like the bird itself, commands our respect. —ROB PALMER

Ferruginous Hawk

The scientific name for the Ferruginous Hawk is *Buteo regalis*, Royal Hawk—fitting for the largest hawk in North America and perhaps the most regal. —ROB PALMER

The Ferruginous Hawk has a huge gape and is able to open its mouth very wide, with the rear edge extending way back on the head below the eye. This might allow them to swallow huge prey items at once—beneficial since they live in open country where raptors like Golden Eagles can spot them at a distance and try to steal their prey. It may also help them dissipate body heat when panting in high temperatures, especially at the exposed nest. —ROB PALMER

Like so many other buteos, or soaring hawks, these birds are polymorphic, with light, rufous, dark rufous, and dark morphs; there are no subspecies.
—ROB PALMER

A light-colored Ferruginous Hawk, showing the V on the belly formed by the rufous leg feathers, present only on adults.
—ROB PALMER

Dark morph birds are less common, constituting just up to 10 percent of the total population.
—ROB PALMER

A rancher kindly left this nest that was built on hay bales alone, and the hawks successfully fledged three young.
—ROB PALMER

A young Ferruginous Hawk showing the wide gape characteristic of the species. —ROB PALMER

A dark rufous morph Ferruginous Hawk launches from a fence post. —ROB PALMER

The chick on the right is engulfing a large rodent. —NICK DUNLOP

Siblings await a meal. Although young females are larger, young males develop sooner and may leave the nest as much as ten days before their sisters. —ROB PALMER

A cliff nest in Wyoming. Once this chick fledges it will take about a month for it to become skilled at flying; hunting finesse will take even longer. —ROB PALMER

Although these chicks may not look like it now, as adults they will be spectacular and formidable predators of the open skies. Ferruginous Hawks are another true Raptor of the West, nesting in seventeen U.S. states and three provinces of Canada. —NICK DUNLOP

Nick Dunlop reports that this Ferruginous Hawk nest in western Nevada and others he has observed are always nearly immaculate, with no prey remains strewn about. As the chicks get older, they swallow everything whole. At this nest mice were a favorite prey item. —NICK DUNLOP

Exercise at the nest begins with short walks and wing flaps to build strength. —ROB PALMER

Ferruginous Hawks sometimes nest on the ground, and probably did so more frequently in the past. Before fire suppression and shelterbelts, trees were less common in this bird's preferred open habitat. Main nesting materials have also changed, as historically bison bones and fur were often used. —ROB PALMER

A nesting site that has been used for years, perhaps by generations of Ferruginous Hawks. Nesting material has blown out or been dislodged by the growing young, coming to rest at the base of the outcropping. —ROB PALMER

Nests are usually completely exposed to the elements and offer sweeping views of the surrounding countryside. They are often built on a prominent feature in the landscape: single trees, cliff faces, rocky outcrops, and utility poles and towers. —ROB PALMER

The common name of the Ferruginous Hawk comes from the Latin word *ferrugo*, meaning "iron rust." This magnificent adult certainly lives up to its name. —ROB PALMER

Male American Kestrels sport slate gray upper wings, a buffy upper breast, and spots on the belly. Sexes are easily identified by plumage even as young in the nest—unique for a falcon species. —KATE DAVIS

Female Kestrels are as much as 10 percent larger than males, lack the gray upper wings, and have a heavily barred tail. —ROB PALMER

Hovering requires the largest energy expenditure of any mode of flight, taking four times the energy of level flight. In spite of this Kestrels often hover over hunting ground, especially if no perches are present, facing into the wind, then gliding to another spot to continue hovering. —ROB PALMER

As secondary cavity nesters, American Kestrels use woodpecker holes, as well as natural hollows in trees, eaves of buildings, crevices on cliffs and even dirt banks and old magpie nests. This female is bringing in a big, fat caterpillar. —ROB PALMER

Insects, like this cricket, are a major portion of the American Kestrel's diet, which also include grasshoppers, beetles, dragonflies, and cicadas, depending on availability. Small rodents, such as mice and voles, are another important food source. The smaller males are more apt than the females to catch songbirds, especially in the winter. —NICK DUNLOP

In 1925, ornithologist William Brewster described the American Kestrel as "most lighthearted and frolicsome." —ROB PALMER

As cavity nesters, American Kestrels are attracted to human-made boxes, and ambitious projects to increase their numbers have resulted in interesting research. As an example, when nest boxes were placed on the back of interstate highway signs, the young fledged away from the busy traffic with very few auto mortalities. —ROB PALMER

American Kestrels are primarily sit-and-wait hunters, dashing out when prey is spotted. Black spots on the rear of the head and neck of both sexes are called ocelli. These "false eyes" may discourage a predator that is approaching from behind in an attempt to steal prey from the falcon, as it appears to be looking right at the potential thief and thus the element of surprise is lost. —ROB PALMER

Kestrels often pump their tails, especially when landing. They bob their heads often while observing potential prey (or predators). This is called motion parallax, and it allows the bird to better judge depth and distance by observing the object from a variety of angles. —ROB PALMER

A stoop, or steeply angled dive, after prey—headfirst at rodents and feetfirst at insects. —ROB PALMER

The American Kestrel is a colorful resident of open country across the continent, the most widespread of the North American falcons, and appreciated by all who enjoy their sharp *killy killy* call and aerial acrobatics.
—KATE DAVIS

California Condor

The decorative ruff of feathers around the neck of the California Condor seems fitting for such an avian celebrity, which was extinct in the wild for five years. Captive breeding and reintroduction have saved one of the most endangered birds in the world—for now at least. —NICK DUNLOP

This bird at a sea lion haul-out in Big Sur, California, hopes a carcass will wash up. The California Condor's range formerly extended across much of North America before the late Pleistocene die-offs of the giant mammoths, camels, and ground sloths on which they fed. —NICK DUNLOP

California Condors are about the same size as their South American counterpart, the Andean Condor. Weights pushing 30 pounds and wingspans of nearly 10 feet make them larger than any eagle and unmistakable, not to be confused with anything else in flight—except maybe an aircraft! —NICK DUNLOP

In 1987, with numbers in the wild of just twenty-one individuals, the executive decision was made to capture every remaining condor. Captive breeding at several facilities with different organizations has been very successful, and the first young were reintroduced in 1992 in California and 1996 in Arizona. In April of 2002, the first chick was hatched in the wild in eighteen years. —NICK DUNLOP

As of September 2010, 192 California Condors existed in the wild—94 in California, with the rest in Arizona near the Grand Canyon. Pairs breed at about six to eight years of age, are monogamous, and remain together year-round. There is only one egg per clutch. —NICK DUNLOP

With such a low breeding rate (one egg per clutch), excessive mortality through shooting and poisoning was nearly the death knell for the species. Especially hazardous is ingesting lead fragments from spent ammunition found in game carcasses and gut piles during hunting season. —NICK DUNLOP

Since 2008, nonlead ammunition is required where condors exist in California. Condors themselves were shot during the gold rush, with the hollow quills of their flight feathers valued for storing gold dust. —NICK DUNLOP

Nearly all California Condors are marked with wing tags and outfitted with telemetry, or radio tracking, setups. The exceptions are the wild-hatched young that embody the success of the reintroduction efforts. —NICK DUNLOP

Rivers and Wetlands

Bald Eagles can be gregarious, especially in the winter. This is a scenic image from Montana, but in this case the birds are probably near a road-killed deer.
—KATE DAVIS

Rivers and streams, ponds and lakes, bogs and marshes, riparian areas—aquatic habitats are richest in overall species diversity. Water fuels the system and draws in predator and prey alike. Many riparian raptors are conspicuous, taking in the sights from a prominent perch or in coursing flight over the landscape.

Ospreys absolutely need live fish, so they are never far from water, nesting in plain view on top of snags, utility poles, metal power towers, and nesting platforms, safe from nest-raiding raccoons. Although not as dependent on fish as the Osprey, the Bald Eagle has become an increasingly common sight on waterways, perching out in the open for all to admire, an icon of the environmental ethic. Nothing

can panic a flock of waterbirds like a Peregrine Falcon, with ducks holding tight on a pond, fearful of taking to the air and becoming a target. Flocks of shorebirds may be seen shifting and dodging with a falcon in hot pursuit.

Formerly called a Marsh Hawk, the Northern Harrier's wandering, buoyant, and tilting flight belies its true speed and predatory skills—catching birds in the air and prey on the ground up to the size of a rabbit. Camouflaged in the grass may be the nest of a Short-eared Owl, with young birds sitting tight and older siblings of various ages hiding far away as a precaution against other predators. Water attracts a wide variety of wildlife, often providing a jackpot for the bird enthusiast.

Northern Harrier

Harriers are described as looking owl-like due to the ruff of feathers that make up the facial disc. Juvenile birds resemble the adult female for the first year. Young males have pale gray or brown irises; females, like this one, have darker brown eyes and are larger in size, about 50 percent heavier. Her eyes will lighten as she gets older, and the male's will become lemon yellow. —KATE DAVIS

As adults, the sexes are so different that they may look like separate species. Males are gray, like the one pictured, and females are brown. Males are practically the only ones out and about in the spring as the females are secretly incubating eggs and brooding young. Northern Harriers are ground nesters, usually in dense grass and vegetation. —KATE DAVIS

A female Northern Harrier. Both sexes have a distinct white rump formed by bright white upper tail coverts. —ROB PALMER

The genus *Circus*, the harriers, is a successful group worldwide. Called a Hen Harrier in Europe and Asia, the Northern Harrier ranges all across the Northern Hemisphere. Judging from the missing wing and tail feathers, this hawk appears to have gotten into a fight or some kind of trouble. —KATE DAVIS

Northern Harriers are famous for their inclination to practice polygyny. Although males are usually monogamous, they may mate with several females in a season, even as many as five or more. Polygyny is largely related to prey abundance. —ROB PALMER

The male provides food for the female and chicks until the young are old enough to maintain body temperature, then the female resumes hunting.
—ROB PALMER

Northern Harriers are partial migrants, with some individuals moving south for the winter and others staying in the same general area year-round. Those that do leave the breeding grounds do so with active flapping flight, feeding along the way and even flying in light rain and snow. Young birds, like this one, may leave a month before the adults.
—ROB PALMER

Hawks and falcons are often very playful, described by Leslie Brown and Dean Amadon as engaging in "actions which seem to reflect an exuberance of physical well-being or vitality, carried out without any immediate biological goal." This adult male harrier was carrying, dropping, and catching a cow pie.
—ROB PALMER

Harriers are known to chase prey on foot and even drown larger animals in irrigation ditches. In winter, they may share communal roosts on the ground.
—ROB PALMER

Northern Harriers are most active at dawn and dusk. The young, like this one at sunset, have a rich orange tinge to their plumage, with just the upper breast streaked. —ROB PALMER

As with owls, the Northern Harrier's facial disc helps direct sound to the ear openings. The Harrier uses its keen hearing as it listens for prey rustling in the grass and brush. —Rob Palmer

Pete Dunne, David Sibley, and Clay Sutton nickname the Northern Harrier the Great Fooler, claiming that its seemingly leisurely flight style is deceptive. Although it typically plugs along, quartering fields and marshes with wings raised in a little V (a dihedral angle), it is capable of astonishing speed and aerial maneuvers. —ROB PALMER

Bald Eagle

Bald Eagles are beyond mere birds to many people. Often called American Eagles, their images are linked to flags and fireworks, patriotism and pride, and military might. —NICK DUNLOP

Adults are instantly recognizable—not really bald but topped with white feathers that match the white tail and tail coverts. —NICK DUNLOP

The solid white head and tail are attained by some young birds around the fifth year, but mostly in the sixth year. This bird has one more year until molting to definitive, or adult, plumage; Bald Eagles rarely breed before then. The beak, cere (fleshy base of the beak), and eye color also change from dark brown to yellow as the birds mature. —ROB PALMER

The Bald Eagle is one of eight species of sea eagles of the genus *Haliaeetus*, and not surprisingly it tends to favor fish over mammals and birds. But in the words of biologist David Buehler, "It often scavenges prey items when available, pirates food from other species when it can, and captures its own prey as a last resort." —NICK DUNLOP

This strikingly marked bird is in its third year. Northern Bald Eagle populations have always been high, and bounties were even paid in Alaska because fisherman feared (falsely) that the birds would affect their salmon catch. South of the 40th parallel, the species was affected by the widespread and vigorous use of the pesticide DDT after World War II, and Bald Eagles were declared endangered in 1967. —NICK DUNLOP

Northern coastal birds are year-round residents, but Bald Eagles from inland Alaska and Canada migrate south, some as far as the Mexican border, in September and October, returning the following March. Most in the Lower 48 also stay put all year, although most youngsters travel north into Canada soon after fledging. —ROB PALMER

Population numbers have increased since DDT was banned in the United States in 1972, and Bald Eagles were removed from the Endangered Species List in 2007. They made it back on their own with only protective measures taken; no captive birds were bred for reintroduction. —KATE DAVIS

Two young Bald Eagles scrap over this appealing piece of real estate on the Washington coast. Foraging on carrion such as roadkill is common in young birds, and for the entire population of Bald Eagles over the winter. Despite claims to the contrary, there are very few documented instances of them killing livestock, such as a newborn lambs. —NICK DUNLOP

Eagles take a long time to reach maturity, but adults have a relatively low mortality rate and can be long-lived, making it to twenty and rarely thirty years of age. Pair bonds may last a lifetime; nonmigratory pairs often associate year-round, whereas migrants get reacquainted at the nest site. —ROB PALMER

Rob Palmer has taken an amazing series of photographs of Bald Eagles catching starlings and blackbirds in the air over a feedlot in Colorado. The owners were using a neurotoxin to try to control the starlings and blackbirds, and Palmer suspects that caused them to fly erratically and become targets for the waiting eagles. —ROB PALMER

No, this is not a flying fish, but one dropped by an adult eagle that was being harassed by this youngster, who scored a free meal. Ospreys in particular are tormented by Bald Eagles and often relinquish their catch. —ROB PALMER

A young Bald Eagle catches a Red-winged Blackbird in an image that won the 2009 BBC/Violea bird behavior category—first place out of 43,000 entries. —ROB PALMER

Bald Eagle nests are some of the largest in the world, usually in prominent trees overlooking water. This nest in Montana has consistently fledged three birds instead of the normal two, with the youngsters lingering in the nest until the age of about eighty days and practicing flight skills with hops and flaps, sometimes landing on the roof of a nearby house.
—KATE DAVIS

At one point in the mid-1970s only twelve Bald Eagle nests could be found in the state of Montana. Forty years later, over four hundred pairs are breeding, a steady population increase of about 10 percent a year. It remains to be seen when the numbers will plateau.
—KATE DAVIS

Bald eagles pluck fish from the water close to the surface. They also take waterfowl, especially when lakes and rivers ice up and prevent them from catching fish. Bald Eagles are also capable of capturing birds up to the size of a goose in the air. —ROB PALMER

A huge and impressive raptor, the Bald Eagle is only found in North America. As a true American native, it was chosen by Congress to be the U.S. national emblem in 1782, despite the protest by Benjamin Franklin, who wanted to pick the Wild Turkey. —ROB PALMER

Where food sources are plentiful, Bald Eagles congregate in numbers up to one thousand individuals, especially in the winter. These birds were at Farmington Bay, Utah, at a wildlife management area that induces a big fish die-off in late January, attracting hundreds of eagles and photographers alike. —ROB PALMER

The 2009 Audubon Grand Prize winner of Bald Eagles battling in Utah. The eagle below had just dropped a fish on the ice so he could roll over and protect himself from a mugging. The attacking bird stole the fish. —ROB PALMER

Short-eared Owl

The well-defined facial disc of the Short-eared Owl hints at the acute hearing it uses to locate scurrying rodents. Stiff feathers surround each eye and amplify sound, directing it to the ear openings. —ROB PALMER

As ground nesters, Short-eared Owls are especially vulnerable to predators. Chicks grow quickly and triple in weight the first five days, tripling again over the next five days. With circuitous flights to deliver prey, adults disguise the location of the nest to other predators (and photographers).
—ROB PALMER

Their tawny streaks and buffy, cryptic coloration allow Short-eared Owls to roost and nest in the grass undetected. When snow completely covers the ground, they move up into trees, and often roost communally in large numbers over the fall and winter. —ROB PALMER

While Short-eared Owls are mainly nocturnal, they can be active at any time of time of day, including dawn and dusk, depending on the season and available prey. The male performs spectacular courtship displays, visible for quite a distance, showing off his territory. With undulating flights he claps his wings below him to drop "like a stone." —ROB PALMER

Short-eared Owls are deadly on rodents, primarily voles and lemmings. Cosmopolitan birds, they occur on every continent except Australia and Antarctica, with a single, uniform-appearing subspecies, *Asio flammeus flammeus*, across North America, Europe, and Asia. —ROB PALMER

As with other owls, the "ears" of a Short-eared Owl are not ears at all but feather tufts originating above the inside corner of each eye. Usually hidden, the short tufts are erected when the owl is agitated or investigating an intruder. —ROB PALMER

This owl was one of eight that waited until the last minute to fly as the photographer marched through the grass with a trained Peregrine overhead. The falcon paid no attention, and this owl dove back into cover a hundred yards ahead. —KATE DAVIS

The flight of the Short-eared Owl is often described as mothlike and buoyant. It can be distinguished from a harrier by the short head and tail, and lack of a white rump. Barred wingtips and a black carpal patch are present on dorsal and ventral surfaces of the wing. —ROB PALMER

OPPOSITE PAGE: A Short-eared Owl springs into flight. Short-eared Owls may be observed flying hundreds of feet aloft, sometimes a dozen individuals together. As described by Hans Peeters, they "engage in a stately airborne ballet that looks oddly formal as they glide about one another in arcs." —ROB PALMER

Long ear tufts occur only in nocturnal owl species, perhaps serving to break up the silhouette and making them harder to spot as they roost in trees. Because the Short-eared Owl is diurnal and generally not a tree rooster, it may not benefit as much from long ear tufts mimicking broken twigs. —ROB PALMER

Short-eared Owls have benefited from the protection of critical waterfowl habitat by such groups as the U.S. Fish and Wildlife Service and Ducks Unlimited, breeding and hunting rodents in wetland landscapes. —ROB PALMER

Osprey

The Osprey is a rare bird in the literal sense: a one-of-a-kind creature. In its own family, Pandionidae, with one species that lives worldwide, it is a raptor with unique physical traits and breeding strategies. This young Osprey has the orange (or red) eyes and light feather edges that indicate it is under one year of age. —KATE DAVIS

Ospreys are piscivores, catching and eating live fish, which make up 99 percent of their diet. A note to trout anglers— in most areas their diet is largely rough fish like suckers, carp, and squawfish, plus whitefish, sunfish, and perch. —ROB PALMER

Ospreys lack the bony ridge over the eye that gives eagles and hawks their fierce appearance. Ospreys instead have a "feline" look. —ROB PALMER

Especially lengthy legs allow Ospreys to grab fish in the water. Their long, narrow wings are efficient for hovering while spotting fish below. Ospreys are so powerful that they can take off, often with a large fish in their talons, after being fully submerged—a feat most other raptors find impossible. —ROB PALMER

Hunting Ospreys cover a lot of ground—or water, actually— coursing back and forth searching for fish near the surface or in the shallows. When necessary, Ospreys are able to plunge underwater to a depth of up to 3 feet to snag a meal. —ROB PALMER

Power companies are often more than happy to install alternative nest sites rather than have bulky stick nests short out electrical lines. This Osprey family atop a platform installed next to a riverside patio entertains residents at a rest home in Montana. —KATE DAVIS

Ospreys are very atypical for raptors in that the young migrate to the wintering grounds and remain there until they are three years old. They first breed at between three and five years of age. Adults, which form long-term pair bonds and have a life span of fifteen to twenty-five years, return each year to breed at or near the place they were born. —ROB PALMER

Osprey populations crashed in many areas of North America in the 1950s to 1970s due in large part to poisoning from the pesticide DDT. The chemical was banned in 1972, and today their numbers have rebounded to historical levels across much of North America. Their recovery was also thanks to their use of artificial platforms for nesting and their tolerance of human activity. —ROB PALMER

Diving headfirst, then feetfirst, an Osprey goes in for the catch. The outer toes are reversible, moving backward to form a "square" of talons. Osprey nostrils are collapsible, closing on impact with the water, and the bottoms of the feet are rough, with spicules, or spines, to help keep slippery fish from escaping. —MIGUEL LASA

After securing a fish, an Osprey usually holds it with one foot in front of the other with the fish head facing forward for an aerodynamic flight. Some Ospreys even carry fish with them for long-distance water crossings during migration. —MIGUEL LASA

A newly fledged Osprey, still dependent on the adults for food. The brown flecked "necklace" on the breast indicates a female, but not all have this ornamentation. —ERICK GREENE

A boatload of fishermen cheer on a determined Osprey. The old wives' tale of Ospreys drowning by catching fish too big for them is exaggerated. —ROB PALMER

A young Osprey is learning how to fish on its own before the long migration—a big learning curve and a big journey ahead. —ROB PALMER

A cosmopolitan denizen of the world, the Peregrine Falcon may be the most famous raptor due to its brush with extinction, incredible flight speeds, and, in the last thirty years, familiarity to city dwellers as the raptor that nests high on structures and feasts on urban birds—even at night, illuminated by city lights. —KATE DAVIS

Typical of falcons, Peregrines have the long slender toes so effective in striking and grabbing birds in the air. They prey on over three hundred species of birds in North America, up to the size of the Canada Goose and Sandhill Crane, but mostly stick to smaller birds that they can carry. —ROB PALMER

Peregrines were locally extinct, or extirpated, over nearly their entire range in the Lower 48 and much of Canada from the 1950s to 1970s, falling victim to rampant DDT pesticide use. After a huge reintroduction effort, Peregrine numbers may even surpass historic levels, a successful recovery that took less than thirty years. —ROB PALMER

The Pacific Ocean offers a plethora of prey items. This Peregrine took advantage of sea and shorebirds, as well as inland perching birds like meadowlarks.
—NICK DUNLOP

A young of the Peales's subspecies carries a partially eaten gull, rescuing her meal from Bald Eagle kleptoparasites that fancied it for themselves.
—ROB PALMER

A Tundra Peregrine in migration, later captured and banded by researchers from Coastal Raptors on the Washington Coast. —NICK DUNLOP

This Peregrine has knocked a Mallard drake to the ice, the struggle ending with a bite to the neck and a quick separation of the spinal cord with the tomial tooth, a sharp triangular projection on the falcon's upper beak. —KATE DAVIS

A trained Peregrine is captured in a stoop sequence from several hundred feet after a pheasant flushed from the grass. Diving speeds may top 220 mph in attacks from thousands of feet overhead, a hyper-streamlining body shape allowing the falcon to "slip through the molecules of air," as falconers may describe it, tongue in cheek. —KATE DAVIS

121

A Peregrine takes a bath in freshwater—and not in a little puddle or creek, but in a river flowing into the ocean. —NICK DUNLOP

Peregrines are built for high-speed flight. Their teardrops are especially viscous, making them less likely to dry out, and structures on the inside of the nictitating membrane (third eyelid) brush away debris from the air. Falcon nostrils are round with a boney baffle in the center, which is thought to break up the airflow for breathing in a stoop. —KATE DAVIS

Peregrine means "wanderer," but of the nineteen subspecies worldwide, just a few migrate. These include two of the three subspecies in North America, the Tundra and the Continental. The Northwest coastal Peale's Peregrine, seen here in Washington, is largely sedentary but moves down the coast as far as Central California. —ROB PALMER

This young male Peregrine had fledged a few days earlier, judging from his flying—and landing—skills. Although fledglings need no instruction on the former, the latter takes practice, and youngsters will try to land on sheer faces, leaves on trees, and other unlikely spots before mastering the skill. —KATE DAVIS

123

Peregrines have made dramatic comeback in California, from a low of two known nests in the early 1970s to over 250 pairs today. —NICK DUNLOP

The Continental, or *anatum*, subspecies of Peregrine has a characteristic orangish or salmon cast to the feathers. Adults of the Arctic subspecies, *tundrius*, show a rosy overwash, especially females, before they bleach out in the sun. —KATE DAVIS

Peregrines have colonized major cities across North America since their return from the brink of extinction; many of those urban birds have even quit migrating. The most famous avian resident of San Jose, California, is Clara, who has been nesting on the 18th floor of City Hall since a box was installed in 2006. Her every action is monitored through binoculars, scopes, and a webcam operated by a dedicated group of volunteers who call themselves "Falconatics." —NICK DUNLOP

Panic ensues as a Peregrine appears, racing through a flock of shorebirds in California. Some Peregrines "fixate" on just one or two species, specializing in capturing a certain type of prey. One female was especially adept in hunting these flocks, catching a bird nearly every time. —NICK DUNLOP

A tiercel (male) Peregrine flies across the nest cliff, which is directly above a popular recreational beach. Peregrines seem unperturbed by human activity below them but might abandon a breeding site if humans are above them. —KATE DAVIS

Fledgling Peregrines in coastal California, "brownies" that will remain with the parents for up to a month. They will spend hours a day in play, flying around the cliff in mock battles and chases, honing their flight skills. —NICK DUNLOP

A coastal California Peregrine family has used this old raven nest for years, the sticks belying the fact that falcons never build their own structures. Imagine the screams from these hungry babies—deafening! —NICK DUNLOP

Nick Dunlop has observed and photographed perhaps the most amazing predatory tactics in the world: falcons attacking immense flocks of starlings in central California. Tens of thousands of these birds flock up every few years, feeding on the ground until the falcon is spotted, when they take to the air in swirling clouds, funnels, and ribbons. One can imagine the Peregrine catching a starling in each foot every time, but Nick reports that relatively few of these attacks were productive. The prey birds are packing in tightly and turning in unison, confusing the falcon with so many options. —NICK DUNLOP

In the wine country of California, managers of vineyards must surely wish that more of these predators were present to assist with the seemingly insurmountable task of controlling the avian menace of starlings, a nonnative pest. —NICK DUNLOP

129

Woodlands and Forest Edges

A young Northern Goshawk on the hunt. —KATE DAVIS

If we are lucky enough to catch a glimpse of a raptor darting back into the cover of a forest, we may have to play back the image in our heads to relive and enjoy, as it might have been ever so brief. Often this is as we are driving and concentrating on more serious matters than bird identification, but it's always a thrill to spot a bird, whether perched or cruising the skies.

In much of the American West, temperate coniferous forests dominate, with deciduous forests an important component. Woodlands, open forests, and forest edges contain a mix of trees, shrubs, and grasses that are home to a great variety of wildlife and offer birds of prey abundant opportunities for hunting and nesting.

The Red-tailed Hawk is probably the most familiar raptor, widespread and conspicuously perched in rural settings or floating over fields across the country. The Red-shouldered Hawk is especially vocal in the breeding season and can be heard year-round with its high-pitched, shrill call, drawn out and repeated both when perched or flying. Especially aerial,

the White-tailed Kite is spotted in open country, facing into the wind and hovering, scouting the ground for game. Turkey and Black Vultures, with their seemingly effortless circles over the terrain, grab our attention from miles away. A little falcon with dazzling flight, perhaps flying away with a bird in its grips, could be a Merlin. With a steady wing beat punctuated with a glide, it's probably a Northern Goshawk, which a biologist in 1930 called "one of the deadliest, handsomest, bravest birds of prey in the world."

The nighttime forays and hoots and shrieks of the ubiquitous Great Horned Owl are often an entry-level experience for people who will become hooked on birds of prey for life. Barn Owls often occupy abandoned buildings, with a haunting flight out a window at dusk. A Northern Pygmy-Owl might frequent the bird feeder in the winter, taking advantage of the smorgasbord of avian selections—after all, that's why they call it a bird feeder, right? Many of these species of raptors are familiar to bird enthusiasts and others require some effort to find—or pure luck.

Chances are that just about everyone who has ever been out of the city in North America has seen a Red-tailed Hawk whether they knew it or not. Red-tails are found in just about every habitat that has a perch for hunting. —KATE DAVIS

The *kreeee* call of a Red-tailed Hawk is synonymous with wilderness in so many television commercials or films, often attributed to a different species (usually a Bald Eagle) or to another continent altogether.
—KATE DAVIS

These hawks occasionally molt into the namesake red tail by the end of their first year of age, but more typically during the second. In flight, the dark leading edge of the wing is easy to spot in the field. —ROB PALMER

Red-tailed Hawks are highly variable in plumage coloration. This is a typical Western variety with light breast and darker belly, or cummerbund; a young female, she sports the huge feet of the larger sex. —KATE DAVIS

While it may look like a light morph or subspecies, this Western Red-tail is actually leucistic, an individual with reduced pigmentation. It spent years as a local attraction for birdwatchers and photographers in Colorado. —ROB PALMER

Mostly preying on mammals, Red-tailed Hawks also take birds such as pheasants and quail. In typical raptor fashion, they hide their food by mantling, or spreading the wings and tail to cover their catch, constantly glancing up and looking around when thieves are present. —KATE DAVIS

From left, a Ferruginous Hawk, a Rough-legged Hawk, another Ferruginous Hawk, and a Red-tail are all on the lookout for mammals in the snow of Nevada. —NICK DUNLOP

Red-tailed Hawks are hugely successful even in this day and age. They are tolerant of humans and many of the alterations to the environment, adaptive and generalist in feeding and breeding. —ROB PALMER

Red-tailed hawks do most of their hunting out in the open, kiting and soaring, although they also hunt from elevated perches, cliffs, trees, and utility poles. —ROB PALMER

Like many hawks, not all Red-tailed Hawks migrate: birds in the north generally migrate each fall, while those in the south do not. Some Northern Red-tails stick it out and don't migrate, often dependent on weather and prey availability. Red-tailed Hawks in southern latitudes may share their territory all winter with Northern migrants that do make it that far south. —KATE DAVIS

Researchers attach numbered aluminum leg bands to birds caught in nets or captured as nestlings, such as this Red-tailed Hawk. Although only about 8 percent of banded raptors are encountered and reported, a great deal of scientific information is collected, especially on movements, life span, and causes of mortality. —ROB PALMER

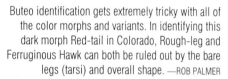

Buteo identification gets extremely tricky with all of the color morphs and variants. In identifying this dark morph Red-tail in Colorado, Rough-leg and Ferruginous Hawk can both be ruled out by the bare legs (tarsi) and overall shape. —ROB PALMER

A close encounter of the falconry kind: a trained Peregrine scraps with a wild young Red-tail. Perhaps the hawk thought the falcon was carrying something to eat. Either way, they grasped each other's feet, swung around once, and parted—the entire encounter lasting just a few seconds. —KATE DAVIS

A well-fed nestling at just over one month of age. Not all young Red-tails are so fortunate; siblings that miss feedings when food is scarce will be stunted, and may be killed and even eaten by healthier nest mates (a behavior known as siblicide or fratricide). —KATE DAVIS

Red-tailed Hawks nest high in sites from trees to cliffs, as in the case of this pair. The eggs are laid every other day and incubation begins with the first one. Hatching is asynchronous, one at a time, so nestlings run the gamut in ages and sizes. —ROB PALMER

Nonmigratory Red-tailed Hawk
pairs remain together year-round.
—NICK DUNLOP

140

Merlin

Researcher Bruce Haak calls the Merlin, like this Prairie Merlin, the "perfect predator, unequaled ounce for ounce in speed, power, aggression, and adaptability." —ROB PALMER

Three subspecies occur in North America. The Taiga or Boreal Merlin is the most northern and most migratory, with individuals from Alaska making it to South America for the winter. Other subspecies are Black or Pacific Merlins, which breed in the Pacific Northwest, and Prairie or Richardson's Merlins, which breed in the northern Great Plains. —NICK DUNLOP

Juvenile birds of either sex look like their mothers, with brown plumage. Males differentiate at one year, with blue-gray upper parts, but are always smaller than females. This is a male Prairie Merlin. —ROB PALMER

Merlins were formerly called Pigeon Hawks, mostly because they resemble pigeons in size and in flight. They are capable of killing pigeons but mostly feed on songbirds; waxwings and House Sparrows are favorites. This is a Taiga Merlin. —NICK DUNLOP

Merlins, like this Prairie, enjoy harassing other raptors that invade their personal space, not just around a nest but any time of the year, often chasing the offending hawks, falcons, or eagles for long distances. —ROB PALMER

Domed stick nests of magpies are commonly used by Merlins (like this Prairie Merlin), often found in an isolated shrub, tree, or shelterbelt far from any other cover or even a water source. They also use hawk and crow nests, tree cavities, and rock ledges. —ROB PALMER

Merlins have been observed getting close to unwary flocks of birds by imitating the flight of a harmless woodpecker or songbird. In they come, with a bouncing flap and glide, and by the time the prey birds realize it's a Merlin, such as this Prairie Merlin, it's often too late. —ROB PALMER

The largest of the three subspecies, Prairie Merlins are lighter in color than other Merlins and have four white tail bands plus white tips on the tail feathers. —ROB PALMER

Merlins can approach prey birds by using vegetation and terrain to mask their approach, pouring on the speed at the end. They also make steep angled dives, like this Prairie Merlin, or chase larks, spiraling upwards in the "ringing flight" that made them so popular in falconry with Medieval ladies of the court. —ROB PALMER

Taiga Merlins have three light bands on the tail and may interbreed with the other subspecies where ranges overlap, with offspring sharing characteristics of both. —ROB PALMER

Prairie Merlins have benefited from expanding urban landscapes, thanks in large part to ornamental berry trees that attract waxwings. Along with House Sparrows and starlings, these songbirds provide an abundant food supply. Thus many Prairie Merlin populations have ceased to migrate and become year-round city dwellers. —NICK DUNLOP

Black Merlins are considered to be birds of the humid forests of the Northwest coast. They tend to be nonmigratory, but some individuals venture inland and south to California in the winter. —ROB PALMER

A male Taiga Merlin stretching in California. —NICK DUNLOP

Barn Owl

Even a tiny child can recognize and draw a Barn Owl—the unique heart-shaped facial disc is among several characteristics that set this family (Tytonidae) apart from the "typical" owls (family Strigidae). —ROB PALMER

The Barn Owl ties for the widest world distribution for a land bird, a distinction it shares with the Peregrine Falcon and the Osprey. Each species lives on every continent except Antarctica. —ROB PALMER

Barn Owls are cavity nesters, making use of everything from trees and cliff cavities to human-made structures like barns and bridges. Nesting boxes have been installed for pest-control projects and in conservation efforts where natural sites are lacking. —ROB PALMER

The Barn Owl has the most acute hearing of any animal investigated, easily able to home in on hidden prey. Their flight is silent to human ears. Optimal foraging-flight height is about 10 feet over the hunting ground below. —ROB PALMER

The Barn Owl's diet is the most studied of any raptor species. Regurgitated after each meal, a pellet is a package of undigested bones, fur, feathers, or insect exoskeletons. Researchers can analyze them in extreme detail for information on prey species. —ROB PALMER

Their associations with old buildings (and cemeteries), silent nocturnal flight, unearthly vocalizations, and wide-eyed stare have often left the Barn Owl labeled as bearer of bad luck and death—an unjust characterization given their service in pest control, as well as their place in the heart of those people that collect "anything owl." —ROB PALMER

Barn Owls typically capture prey by diving headfirst, at the last moment throwing out their lethal talons, forming a square with two talons in front and two in back to firmly grasp their prey. They also pursue prey on foot occasionally.
—ROB PALMER

Small mammals make up from three-quarters to all of the Barn Owl's diet. Researchers have calculated the benefits of this diet as follows: in a ten-year lifespan at 90 grams of food a day, a single Barn Owl would eat about eleven thousand mice, far more effective to the farmer than rodenticides and even fertilizers, and free of cost! —ROB PALMER

Northern Goshawk

Young Northern Goshawks have white eyebrows, a trait for life. Their irises change from greenish gray to pale yellow to bright yellow, like this one-year-old male's, eventually becoming deep red at maturity. Red eyes and gray plumage with fine black barring indicate an adult. —NICK DUNLOP

The relatively short wings, long tail, and amazing reflexes allow the accipiters (forest hawks) to boldly dash through foliage chasing prey. The largest member of this group, the Northern Goshawk, is valued in falconry for its strength, persistence, and nerve. It is nicknamed the "cook's hawk" for its ability to kill game and provide food. —KATE DAVIS

The male provides nearly all of the food for the incubating and brooding female and chicks, although she often can't resist killing prey that ventures near the nest. He delivers the food and then is expected to leave, or leaves after she gives her "dismissal" call. —NICK DUNLOP

arents add layers of green limbs to the chosen nest to advertise to other ptors that it is being used and to thwart pathogens and parasites. A gh, closed forest canopy, usually with water in the form of a stream or ke nearby, is a characteristic choice for a nest site. —ROB PALMER

With up to eight nests in their territories, Northern Goshawks keep researchers guessing which one they will use each spring. These site swaps may cut down on parasites and disease. —ROB PALMER

Goshawks hunt in forests and along forest edges using a short-duration sit-and-wait tactic, flying from perch to perch in search of hares and rabbits, squirrels, grouse, and corvids like crows and jays. —ROB PALMER

Goshawks also chase down birds in flight, stalk prey on foot, and crash through thick brush— seemingly undaunted in all situations. —ROB PALMER

A wintering juvenile Northern Goshawk in Wyoming. —ROB PALMER

Northern Pygmy-Owl

This Northern Pygmy-Owl played an important role as an educator for Raptors of the Rockies for over ten years. We called him DotCom and he was a program favorite, with the most common question being, "Is that how big they are?" —KATE DAVIS

Once they spot their potential prey, Northern Pygmy-Owls hop from limb to limb, zigzagging and flicking their tail back and forth, completely absorbed in the attack. They may also fly like an accipiter, with several flaps and a glide. Finally they fly straight down or at a steep angle and pounce, using their relatively large feet and talons to squeeze the prey, puncturing its vital organs. —BT "TAD" LUBINSKI

This Pygmy-Owl was mobbed by a wren and hummingbird, potential prey birds that were noisily alerting their compatriots that a predator was in their midst. Birdwatchers are often rewarded with a raptor if they follow the calls of mobbing songbirds. —KATE DAVIS

False eyes (ocelli) on the back of the head may keep mobbing birds from getting too close, giving the impression that the owl is looking right at them. They also may fool a kleptoparasite that hopes to steal a Pygmy-Owl's meal. —KATE DAVIS

The "tooting" call of the Northern Pygmy-Owl is slower and lower than that of the Saw-whet Owl, but equally monotonous and repetitive. —GERALD ROMANCHUK

Northern Pygmy-Owls are polymorphic, appearing grayish in the Rocky Mountains (like this bird), brown on the Pacific Coast, and rufous in their southern range of Mexico and Central America. —KATE DAVIS

Large prey items can't be carried away, so Northern Pygmy-Owls cache uneaten portions nearby, or simply return to the kill later to resume feeding. —KATE DAVIS

The Northern Pygmy-Owl is a powerful predator capable of killing birds and mammals twice its size. Pygmy-Owls are very approachable by people and are active during the day. Moving down into valleys in the winter, they often frequent bird feeders, putting on a show for human onlookers. —KATE DAVIS

Turkey Vulture / Black Vulture

Along with Black Vultures and California Condors, Turkey Vultures belong to the New World Vultures, not closely related to Old World Vultures but sharing many characteristics because of the same scavenging lifestyle—a classic case of convergent evolution, where species independently evolve similar traits. Necessary custodians of the landscape, Turkey Vultures feast mainly on dead animals, including fish. —ROB PALMER

Turkey Vultures hold their wings in a dihedral, like a shallow V, contributing to being known among birdwatchers as TV. Golden Eagles also hold their wings in a dihedral in flight, but eagles do not tilt from side to side as TVs do. —NICK DUNLOP

Black Vultures may be confused with young Turkey Vultures but have a shorter tail and flatter wing profile when flying. —ROB PALMER

Black Vultures, like this one, don't have any sense of smell and may cue in on Turkey Vultures to locate carrion. Although they are smaller, they may outnumber and overwhelm their cousins at a carcass. Black Vultures also roost in great numbers, with hundreds of individuals in one spot. —ROB PALMER

In the recent past researchers had proposed removing New World Vultures from the order of raptors and placing them with the storks. While storks and vultures share many traits, the stork in the old myth of bringing the new baby to human parents will never be replaced by a Turkey Vulture! —ROB PALMER

Despite Turkey Vultures' large numbers and widespread distribution, their breeding strategies are largely a mystery. What is known is that they lay eggs in fallen hollow trees and logs, stumps, ledges, and caves and among tumbled boulders, often on steep slopes. Most research and breeding data has been from studies of nests in abandoned buildings. —ROB PALMER

Turkey Vultures are among the few birds to have a well-developed sense of smell, which they use to locate carrion, even when hidden from sight below a canopy of trees. —KATE DAVIS

All New World Vultures spend time sunning themselves daily with wings outstretched. With a Turkey Vulture's wingspan of up to 6 feet, this makes an impressive sight. —ROB PALMER

White-tailed Kite

White-tailed Kites were thought to be close to extinction in the early twentieth century; instead they adapted to agricultural practices and human development and actually expanded their range, and continue to do so. —NICK DUNLOP

With pointed wings, the White-tailed Kite resembles a falcon in shape and flight. Such a light-colored bird is conspicuous in the open range and grasslands, savannah, and marsh habitats it frequents, and also recently at airports and along freeways. It is easily mistaken for a gull or tern, however, and may be overlooked. —ROB PALMER

The White-tailed Kite rarely hunts from a perch. Instead it hovers over a patch of ground, facing into the wind and scanning below for mice and voles, then gliding to the next spot to resume the search. —NICK DUNLOP

The term *kiting*, meaning remaining stationary on the wing in the wind, takes on a new meaning once you've seen an expert in the air. With wings held in a dihedral (shallow V), they are graceful, buoyant, and acrobatic. —NICK DUNLOP

Outside of breeding season, White-tailed Kites are gregarious birds, with some roosts numbering over one hundred individuals. Though not considered migratory, they do become nomadic in search of California voles, rodents whose numbers fluctuate in regular cycles. —NICK DUNLOP

Small prey items are swallowed on the wing, but larger items, like this vole, will be ripped to pieces, with favored bits (like the head) eaten first. The whole time feeding, the kite surveys the vicinity so as not to be surprised by a kleptoparasite. —NICK DUNLOP

White-tailed Kites have a unique tail-bobbing habit, cocking their tail high over their back and moving it up and down, often at the approach of an intruder. As a last resort, they flee. —NICK DUNLOP

Formerly thought to be a subspecies of the Black-shouldered Kite of Africa, Europe, and Asia, White-tailed Kites were split into a separate species in 1994 due to differences in plumage and behavior. The child's toy kite was named for the bird and not the other way around.
—NICK DUNLOP

Great Horned Owl

Great Horned Owls reign supreme, the ultimate avian predator and enemy to all—even other owls. They prey on just about anything they can catch, live anywhere they can find a daytime roost, and nest in the widest array of sites of any raptor in North America. —ROB PALMER

The percentage of people who have actually seen an owl in the wild is anyone's guess, but Great Horned Owls are familiar to all, if not by sight then by their hooting call. Spotting—or hearing—one is often a perfect introduction to the world of birds, and nature in general. —KATE DAVIS

Great Horned Owls breed earlier in the season than most other birds. They usurp an old nest that might be put to use later in the breeding season by the birds that built it in the first place. —ROB PALMER

Babies leave the nest and spread out onto nearby branches before they can fly because a concentration of baby owls might attract another predator. Their nonstop begging may be heard day and night so parents know where they are, but is often difficult for the observer to pinpoint. —ROB PALMER

Great Horned Owls are the nocturnal counterpart of the Red-tailed Hawk with a similar prey base, one taken under the cover of night and the other during the day. Cryptic coloration makes them difficult to see during the day as they quietly roost. At night the only evidence of them might be their deep, resonant hoots, often back and forth between mated pairs. —ROB PALMER

In prairie and grassland landscapes devoid of trees, Great Horned Owls may roost in old buildings and venture out after dark. Unrelated individuals may concentrate in the only tree around for miles, or in an isolated shelterbelt. —ROB PALMER

Great Horned Owls have short, broad wings and powerful flight best suited for slow maneuvers through the trees. They mainly hunt mammals but will take a myriad of animals from invertebrates to skunks—one of the few predators known to eat skunks. They are also any sleeping bird's nightmare. —ROB PALMER

Great Horned Owls don't migrate, even at the most northern latitudes, and are the longest lived of North American Owls. "Your" resident owl pair behind the house will nest year after year, but if one is killed, it will be replaced by a floater, an unmated adult seeking a mate who has suffered such a loss. —KATE DAVIS

As with most raptors, females are larger, and Great Horned Owls are actually the largest owls by weight in the Lower 48, aside from those Snowy Owls that venture down in the winter. Great Gray Owls may be longer but are all feathers when it comes to mass. —KATE DAVIS

Like other owls, Great Horned Owls do not build their own nests and instead take over those of other birds like hawks or crows. They nest most often in trees but also use hollows, old buildings, and, in this case, a cliff ledge in Wyoming. —ROB PALMER

Specialized feather structures give woodland owls the advantage of nearly silent flight. The owl can continue to listen for the scurrying rodent, and prey can't hear the predator's approach—a deadly combination. —KATE DAVIS

Arid-country birds like these are pale, and humid-climate owls are dark, an ecological phenomenon known as Gloger's Rule. Plumage is identical between the sexes and ages of Great Horned Owls. —ROB PALMER

A Great Horned Owl caught in mid-hoot. Even though the females are heavier, their voice is higher in pitch due to a smaller syrinx, or voice box. Her call also has an extra syllable at the beginning, so sexes may be identified in the dark just by voice. —ROB PALMER

These owls nested in the rafters of a barn. The babies' eyes remain closed until about 10 days of age. The mother presents tiny food morsels to the chicks, touching their beaks to stimulate them to feed. Even with eyes closed, they begin snapping their beaks in defense at 6 days. —NICK DUNLOP

Great Horned Owl nests are easy to spot before the leaves appear in the spring. This female's young were nearly ready to fledge as a nearby Red-tailed Hawk pair had just begun courtship. —NICK DUNLOP

Owls are thought to bring the message of death in many cultures, with their mysterious and secretive life and frightening screams in the night. A popular belief these days is the "wise and kind" owl. Either notion is lost on the Great Horned Owl, going about its role as an apex predator. —ROB PALMER

A young Great Horned Owl, not yet ready to fly, scrambles up a branch near its nest.
—ROB PALMER

The Red-shouldered Hawk is common across the eastern half of the United States, with a completely separate population and subspecies in California. Since the mid-1990s their range has expanded to Washington and Baja, and inland even to Arizona. They are seen occasionally in nearly every Western state. —NICK DUNLOP

Red-shouldered Hawks are birds of moist forests, often near open water. They are adapting well to ornamental trees and suburban and urban life.
—ROB PALMER

One of the most vocal of hawks, the Red-shouldered delivers a sharp *kee-aaah* when perched or flying, on territory or elsewhere, at any time. It is also tame and approachable. A young bird is pictured here. —NICK DUNLOP

Red-shouldered Hawk pairs perform flamboyant courtship flights and build or refurbish the nest together, sometimes constructing right on top of another bird's or squirrel's nest. —NICK DUNLOP

With a diet including small mammals, birds (including nestlings), reptiles, crayfish, and insects, Red-shouldered Hawks usually hunt from moderate and low perches. This is a juvenile bird. —ROB PALMER

Red-shouldered Hawks have a leisurely hunting flight, surprising unwitting prey and pursuing whatever happens to cross their path. Generalist feeders, their diet changes from region to region and season to season. Pictured here is the eastern subspecies, seen only occasionally in the West. —ROB PALMER

The Red-shouldered Hawks of southern California are thriving with and despite human encroachment, a staple in planted eucalyptus stands and on freeways. Their eastern counterparts have not adapted so well, for unknown reasons. —NICK DUNLOP

Mature Forests

A Cooper's Hawk waits
for a meal to appear.
—NICK DUNLOP

The forest canopy can hold some surprises. As raptor watchers, we can stumble upon a bit of predation or a nest, or startle a bird that we may not see again in the dense foliage. The mature forest may be parklike with old-growth trees. But more often than not, it can be like a jungle with thick undergrowth and deadfall, so better stick to the trail. Either way, a variety of birds of prey find it just right as a place to thrive.

The true forest hawks are right at home. Sharp-shinned Hawks catch the plentiful songbirds and pluck them at a favorite stump or tree, as evidenced by a pile of feathers. A species that is finding urban settings more attractive for hunting and breeding, the slightly larger Cooper's Hawk quietly slips off a stick nest hidden high in the crotch of a tree.

Woodland owls vocalize to advertise their presence, and the persistent whistling call of the Northern Saw-whet Owl can go on for an hour, with hundreds of whistles in a row.

The Eastern and Western Screech-Owls are separate species but difficult to differentiate where they overlap until they cut loose in song. The Barred Owl has expanded its range westward in the last half century, with riparian forests now punctuated by the nighttime question, "Who cooks for you-all?"

The Spotted Owl is a nocturnal hunter of the mature and old-growth forest and came to symbolize this habitat in the Pacific Northwest. The tiny Flammulated Owl may be more common than once thought but is the epitome of a secretive and solitary species, with cryptic plumage to match. The tall, slender Long-eared Owl similarly blends into its surroundings. At nightfall it is quite the rodent-catching expert, masterfully winding through that thick forest foliage. All of these raptors venture into open country, but observations made in the shadows under the canopy of trees might be more memorable.

Barred Owl

Probably known best for its vocalizations, the Barred Owl's call—likened to "Who cooks for you? Who cooks for you-all?"—penetrates its deep forest and riparian habitats. Barred Owls also engage in wild, caterwauling duets during courtship that can be quite unnerving for a hiker to hear in the dark.
—KATE DAVIS

Barred Owls don't migrate and are territorial year-round, perhaps protecting scarce high-quality nest sites. Here the photographer's flash bounces off the blood vessels in the rear of the eye, causing the same red-eye effect that ruins so many family snapshots. —ROB PALMER

Originally widespread east of the Great Plains, Barred Owls colonized new territories throughout the twentieth century. They first moved northwest into the boreal Canadian forest, then moved south. Barred Owls first arrived in Washington State in 1965; they arrived in California in 1981 and bred there by 1991. —ROB PALMER

arred Owls are generalist feeders, eating mammals, birds, reptiles, and amphibians. hey may chase prey on foot and will wade in shallows for fish. —ROB PALMER

The Barred Owl's expansion may be human-caused. Fire suppression has resulted in more trees and denser forests in the West. They probably moved across the vast, formerly treeless areas of the northern Great Plains by jumping from one planted shelterbelt to the next. —ROB PALMER

Barred Owls are aerial acrobats, weaving through tight limbs and dense foliage in pursuit of prey. Specialized, sound-muffling structures on their feathers—present in most nocturnal woodland owls—allow them to fly silently through the night air. —ROB PALMER

Owls are well-known pellet producers, but more than three hundred other bird species are also known to cough up castings.Prey parts like fur, feathers, and bones can't be digested, so they are processed into balls covered in mucus and regurgitated, one or two a day—like this Barred Owl is about to do. —ROB PALMER

This bird was found hanging in a barbed wire fence as if crucified, barely alive. She was rehabilitated for several weeks and released back at that same spot, flying off and not looking back. —KATE DAVIS

Cooper's Hawk

The medium-sized of the three North American accipiters, in between the smaller Sharp-shinned Hawk and the larger Northern Goshawk, the Cooper's Hawk has a short occipital crest that can be raised to make a square, dark-crowned head. This education program bird, named Alice, lived to be twenty years old, roughly double the longevity of wild hawks. —KATE DAVIS

Although males and females have similar plumage, they can be distinguished by their size, with the female (left) always about one-third larger. Cooper's Hawks in the Northwest are smallest, with a gradual increase in body size farther east. The male provides all the food for his mate, even for the month leading up to egg laying, until well after the young are old enough to self-regulate their body temperature. —ROB PALMER

Of the North American accipiters, the Cooper's Hawk is the most likely to perch out in the open and may be the only one to use utility poles and wires. However, it is usually reclusive, hiding in foliage to dart out after prey in short, swift flights. —ROB PALMER

A female Cooper's Hawk in her first spring, with the brown back and fine streaking on the breast characteristic of juveniles. The legs are of pencil thickness and not little sticks like those of a Sharp-shinned Hawk. —NICK DUNLOP

The short, round wings and long tail are ideal for dashing through vegetation. Cooper's Hawks may usually be distinguished from Sharp-shins by the rounded tail and head jutting far forward of the leading edge of wing. Cooper's Hawks, especially males, spend a lot of time soaring in breeding season. —NICK DUNLOP

189

Juvenal plumage is retained for the first year, and eye color changes from blue-gray in fledglings to yellow the first year. Then it changes to orange and finally red at maturity—more quickly and to a deeper red for the males. —NICK DUNLOP

The eyes of a Cooper's are set well forward on the head, as opposed to centrally in a Sharp-shin. A Cooper's Hawk is an opportunist, pouring on the speed and catching medium-sized birds and mammals, as well as reptiles, in surprise attacks. Although they hunt primarily by sight, they have been known to locate quail solely by hearing their calls. —ROB PALMER

In the East, numbers of Cooper's Hawks dropped dramatically by the mid-twentieth century due to use of the pesticide DDT, but they have made a comeback. Cooper's Hawks have moved into urban landscapes around the country, nesting right in cities and often acting very tame, a bit out of character for a bird thought of as secretive.
—ROB PALMER

Cooper's Hawks sometimes reuse old nests but usually build a new one in the same area with good hunting nearby. The male does most of the construction. One study estimated that the number of copulations per clutch of eggs is 372—probably a record for the bird world.
—ROB PALMER

A crowded house with five young at about three weeks of age (three to five eggs per clutch is typical, with seven being the upper limit). Mortality rates are high, with 72 to 78 percent of the young dying in their first year, mostly from starvation, predation, and accidents. —NICK DUNLOP

This first-year female successfully bred and fledged five young, three of which can be seen in the photo. The other two were out on the limbs. The male provides all of the food for the first half of nesting, bringing smaller prey items from around the vicinity. At this stage the female has resumed hunting, bringing in larger food for the growing young, perhaps from a greater distance. —NICK DUNLOP

Cooper's Hawks were heavily persecuted in the past as "chickenhawks," the nickname coming from the belief that they killed large numbers of domestic birds. That mentality persists today, albeit to a lesser degree thanks to education and federal protection. —ROB PALMER

Northern Saw-whet Owl

The diminutive 8-inch Northern Saw-whet Owl was so named because one of their calls was said to mimic the sound made when sharpening a crosscut saw—a noise common in the olden days when they were so christened. —KATE DAVIS

Saw-whets are rodent catchers, eating their prey in pieces starting with the head. Larger items are consumed in two meals at least four hours apart with the remainder stored in a cache in the tree limbs. Frozen parts of cached prey are thawed out when the owl lies down on them, as if in incubation. —KATE DAVIS

Saw-whet Owls also capture birds, especially perching birds that are caught while migrating at night. Saw-whet Owls like this young bird are very approachable by people and may even be picked up by hand. —KATE DAVIS

Almost completely nocturnal, Saw-whet Owls hunt from low perches from a half hour after sunset until a half hour before sunrise. If prey birds spot one during the day, the owl will be mobbed, surrounded and chastised with scolding calls to alert other songbirds that a predator is in their midst.
—KATE DAVIS

Young birds look very different from adults. Fledged birds remain together, fed by the male for up to a month after leaving the nest cavity.
—GERALD ROMANCHUK

Northern Saw-whet Owls have a repetitive whistled call, very similar to the beeping of a utility truck backing up, and will often respond to an imitation of their call made by people.
—GERALD ROMANCHUK

Spotted Owl

The Spotted Owl is a deep forest resident, with the two Pacific subspecies, Northern and California, reliant on old-growth conifers. The Northern Spotted Owl was listed as threatened in 1990 and became an iconic symbol that completely polarized the timber industry and environmentalist movement in a vehement battle. —NICK DUNLOP

The Mexican Spotted Owl is the third subspecies and also federally listed as threatened. This pair was photographed in Colorado. They prefer mixed conifers, keeping cool in the shade as they roost during the day. —DAVID PALMER

In nighttime hunts Spotted Owls prefer mammals but catch some birds as well. Favorites are flying squirrels in wet coniferous forests and wood rats in mixed conifers, plus mice, voles, rabbits, and hares. —NICK DUNLOP

The call of the Spotted Owl is like an abbreviated version of the call of their close relative, the Barred Owl: "Who are . . . you, you-all?" They also have an array of chitters, whistles, and barks, and can change their vocalizations to imitate other Spotted Owls that are calling. —DAVID PALMER

Spotted Owls are long-lived birds, with some individuals making it to sixteen and seventeen years of age in the wild. Most pairs skip a year or two between nesting, and some refrain for as long as five or six years. —NICK DUNLOP

Barred Owls were formerly eastern birds that have steadily expanded their range westward. More aggressive and versatile than the Spotted Owl, they have displaced their smaller cousin. Hybridization between the two also dilutes the gene pool, and hybrids are fertile, capable of producing offspring.
—NICK DUNLOP

Numbers are down for the Spotted Owl, and their future remains uncertain despite protective legislation and unprecedented scientific research into their habits.
—NICK DUNLOP

Sharp-shinned Hawk

The Sharp-shinned Hawk is the smallest of the three North American accipiters. Females are always larger—to an extreme with these hawks, as males could be half their size. Curiously, there is no overlap in size between males and females of the same species or between different accipiter species. —KATE DAVIS

Sharp-shins have a round head and square tail, and legs with a "sharp" leading edge—obviously named from a dead specimen as the trait is hardly a field mark. —KATE DAVIS

Bulky sticks nests are in a fork or near the tree trunk, hidden in foliage. Both young and adults remain inconspicuous, vulnerable to predation by others due to their small size. —NICK DUNLOP

About 90 percent or more of the Sharp-shinned Hawk's diet is small birds, which they catch by dashing from a perch or by using woodlands to conceal their flight until they surprise their prey. Bird feeders are a major attractant. Plucking posts to plume prey are usually somewhere in the nest vicinity. —ROB PALMER

Although common, Sharp-shinned Hawks are secretive and seldom-seen predators of the forest. They fly with the typical accipiter style, three to six flaps, then a glide—but sped up and flicking compared to a Cooper's Hawk. —ROB PALMER

A female Sharp-shinned Hawk on the lookout, with the round, wide-eyed look of surprise characteristic of the species, along with short white tips on the tail feathers. —ROB PALMER

Flammulated Owl

Flammulated Owls leave the open coniferous forests of western North America to winter in the pine forests of Mexico, where practically nothing is known of their habits. —KATE DAVIS

The tiny Flammulated Owl is completely nocturnal, adept at catching insects like moths, grasshoppers, and beetles in the air. They also glean them from leaves and conifer needles, sometimes while hovering. During the day, their cryptic coloration renders them undetectable, nearly invisible next to the bark of a tree. —KATE DAVIS

Eastern and Western Screech-Owls

The Western Screech-Owl has very subtle characteristics that separate it from its eastern counterpart, including a black bill and a call that sounds like a rubber ball bouncing to a standstill (speeding up at the end). —ROB PALMER

Once considered related subspecies, the Western (pictured here) nd Eastern Screech-Owls were separated into two species in 1983. Nonmigratory, they change their diet with the seasons, eating a great eal of insects over the summer months and switching to more birds nd mammals in the winter. —KATE DAVIS

A roosting Eastern Screech-Owl stands at the entrance to the nest. Its plumage blends into the bark and makes the black nest hole less obvious to a potential predator.
—ROB PALMER

The Eastern Screech-Owl call is a whinny or tremolo, descending in pitch. The call is usually the only way to tell it from a Western where they occur together.
—ROB PALMER

City parks are now favorite haunts of Screech-Owls, perhaps because they are largely free of their enemy, the Great Horned Owl. —ROB PALMER

Long-eared Owl

Similar in markings to Great Horned Owls, Long-eared Owls are smaller and their prominent ear tufts are closer together, originating just over the inside corner of the eye, and standing straight up when the bird is perched. —KATE DAVIS

The cry of a baby Long-eared Owl carries a great distance and sounds like "the noise of a gate with squeaky hinges." —GERALD ROMANCHUK

Both sexes may employ an elaborate tactic for distracting intruders at the nest: they fly right at the offending party, then crash to the ground below the nest, dragging their bodies along the ground with spastic movements, feigning injury, then flying off. —KATE DAVIS

Long-eared Owls have a fast, low, coursing flight over their hunting grounds, punctuated with short glides. Diet is mostly small rodents that they swallow whole; they occasionally surprise roosting birds. Ear tufts are laid back in flight, making them look like Short-eared Owls. —ROB PALMER

Both parents provide food for the young after fledging, but the female eventually disappears and the male continues to feed them on his own for two to three weeks longer. —GERALD ROMANCHU

During courtship the male Long-eared Owl performs a twisting and turning flight through the trees around the nest site, flying over the canopy and clapping his wings below him. This male bird was rehabilitated and released. —KATE DAVIS

Mostly silent the rest of the year, Long-eared Owls in breeding season offer "remarkable" vocalizations, wide in range, with individual birds having their own variations. Typical male calls are a repeated *hoo-hoo-hoo*; others are likened to a bleating lamb, hissing cat, and a dog's barking *woof-woof*.
—GERALD ROMANCHUK

Southwest Specialties

An Aplomado Falcon perched in a yucca in Texas. —NICK DUNLOP

The hot, dry deserts of the southwestern United States provide a unique and challenging habitat for all plants and animals, including raptors. Nights can be cool but daytime temperatures in the summer can soar, regularly exceeding 100 degrees Fahrenheit. The Mojave Desert of southern California, southern Nevada, and northwestern Arizona is the driest, getting 5 or less inches of precipitation per year, all in the winter. The Sonoran Desert, home to the signature saguaro cactus, has two wet seasons, each benefiting its diverse plant and animal communities. The Chihuahuan Desert of southeastern Arizona, southern New Mexico, and southern Texas receives its limited rainfall in the late summer.

Wildlife in these deserts make use of riparian areas at springs and along permanent streams, where cottonwoods and sycamores provide nesting sites for raptors. Numerous mountain ranges rise high above the desolate valleys, providing cooler, forested habitats. What appears to be a barren landscape much of the year comes alive in the spring with flowering plants and breeding birds, many of which are at the northern edge of their range. To see some of these southwestern raptors without leaving the United States, head for natural areas along the southern border, such as Big Bend National Park along the Rio Grande in Texas.

The Harris's is perhaps the most social of the hawks, with groups of a dozen family members hunting together. A raptor wading in a stream after aquatic prey and chasing others on foot is the Common Black Hawk. Gray Hawks are adept at catching spiny lizards from the ground and off tree trunks. What might be mistaken for a Turkey Vulture may be a Zone-tailed Hawk, spending much of the day on the wing with hardly a flap. The Aplomado Falcon was completely gone from the United States by 1952, but this colorful little falcon has been reintroduced in Texas, even nesting on specially designed boxes on poles and yucca. Whiskered Screech-Owls are expert invertebrate catchers, securing crickets, beetles, moths, spiders, and especially centipedes with their tiny talons. The smallest of all, the Elf Owl, is the poster child of the Southwest, poking its head out of its nest hole in a huge saguaro cactus. It's well worth a trip to the region to see the Southwest specialties.

Zone-tailed Hawk

Zone-tailed Hawks often hunt from heights of 300 feet, grabbing birds, lizards, and rodents in a high-speed dive to the ground or tree canopy. —ROB PALMER

Researchers have suggested that by imitating the soaring of harmless carrion-eating vultures, a Zone-tailed Hawk is able to approach unwitting prey below. They may even join vultures in the air and are sometimes difficult even for biologists to casually distinguish. Others believe that gliding on thermals while hunting is simply an energy-efficient way of getting around. —ROB PALMER

Zone-tailed and Common Black Hawks are nearly identical when perched and often occur in the same areas, even nesting side by side. However, the highly aerial Zone-tails spend most of their day on the wing, even more so than Turkey Vultures, with whom they associate. —ROB PALMER

Considered very uncommon in Arizona, Texas, and New Mexico and rare in California, Zone-tailed Hawks need protected nesting areas to prevent their decline. —ROB PALMER

Crested Caracara

The Crested Caracara is said to eat just about any animal material they can find or steal, dead or alive. They will also hunt insects, reptiles, amphibians, birds, and mammals, and many are fond of fish. —ROB PALMER

Also called the Mexican Eagle, the Crested Caracara is the national emblem of Mexico. In soaring flight it resembles an eagle with an oversized head and neck and straight wings. —ROB PALMER

The Crested Caracara is an unusual member of the falcon family, a regal-looking predator that is as at home on the ground as it is in the air, searching out carrion such as roadkill and refuse from dumps, poultry yards, and slaughterhouses. —ROB PALMER

Crested Caracaras differ from true falcons in that they build their own nests, often in the tallest vegetation around. The young are fed more hunted prey, whereas the adults eat a greater percentage of carrion. —ROB PALMER

Crested Caracaras often hang out with vultures, like this Turkey Vulture, waiting for them to rip open large carcasses to feed. Caracaras will also chase the vultures in hopes of forcing the disgorging of a recent meal, often catching the regurgitated meat before it hits the ground.
—ROB PALMER

The fleshy parts on the face and crop of a Crested Caracara quickly change from orange to yellow or bright red when alarmed, usually during conflict with vultures or other caracaras.
—ROB PALMER

Caracaras probably got their musical name, an imitation of their rattling call, from South American Indians. They play an important and historic role in local folklore of Central and South America. —ROB PALMER

Common Black Hawk

Never far from water except during migration, Common Black Hawks specialize in aquatic prey: fish, snakes, amphibians, crabs, and insects. As if hunting aquatic prey in the desert weren't difficult enough, this male in Big Bend National Park in Texas had to cross an open patch of ground guarded fiercely by a Northern Mockingbird every time he made a food delivery to the nest. When he brought in a frog, he barely seemed to notice his brief passenger. —NICK DUNLOP

Common Black Hawks have extremely wide wings and a long tail and legs. They often hunt from a perch or on foot in shallow water. Nests are built in the large cottonwoods and sycamores that line the waterways of the Southwest. —NICK DUNLOP

Elf Owl

Famous for roosting and nesting in giant saguaro, Elf Owls use woodpecker-constructed cavities in just about any tree or cactus available, even hollows in limbs if they afford some relief from the desert heat. This bird was nesting in a cavity in a telephone pole.
—ROB PALMER

The smallest owl in the world, Elf Owls are nocturnal and also highly migratory in their northern range, heading south in the winter because their prey, invertebrates such as insects and spiders, are not as active during the cold nights in the Southwest. They even eat scorpions, after removing the dangerous stinger. —ROB PALMER

In urban areas, Elf Owls have learned to feast upon moths and other insects attracted to bright street and yard lights at night. —ROB PALMER

Gray Hawk

Formerly and colloquially called the Mexican Goshawk, the medium-sized Gray Hawk is often compared to goshawks, or accipiters, in flight, with their flap-flap-glide and maneuverability in foliage. The Gray Hawk is actually a buteo, or soaring hawk, that does very little soaring, staying under the canopy of trees except during courtship flights. —ROB PALMER

The Gray Hawk nests in mature cottonwood stands on river bottoms, a riparian habitat that is increasingly threatened by overgrazing and urban water use. However, they have adapted to these changes by slowly expanding their range into marginal habitats. —ROB PALMER

Gray Hawks skillfully dart and dash after lizards, but they also eat birds, rodents, and large insects. —ROB PALMER

Aplomado Falcon

The Aplomado Falcon gets its name from *plomo*, the Spanish word for "lead," which aptly describes their bluish gray color. Fairly common in the Southwest in the early 1900s, the Aplomado was gone from the United States by 1952 because of habitat destruction. The northern subspecies was listed as federally endangered in 1986, and a captive breeding program has sinced released more than 1,500 birds in Texas and New Mexico. Nick Dunlop spent time with these birds in 2010 at a private ranch in West Texas, photographing falcons released by the Peregrine Fund. —NICK DUNLOP

Similar in size to a Cooper's Hawk, an accipiter to which it is often compared, an Aplomado Falcon can maneuver in tight foliage, hop through limbs, and chase prey on foot. —NICK DUNLOP

Aplomado Falcons catch grassland birds, concentrating on doves and sparrows, but also feed on occasional insects, reptiles, and small mammals, even bats. —NICK DUNLOP

Aplomado Falcons often hunt from the tops of yucca. They frequent water holes and may hunt the perimeters of grass fires, catching fleeing prey. Aplomados like the twilight hours, sometimes hunting before dawn and after sunset. They hide uneaten portions of meals and defend those cache sites against intruders even when no food is present.—NICK DUNLOP

Mated pairs of Aplomados stay together year-round, often perch side by side, hunt cooperatively, and even feed on the same prey. Females may be as much as 45 percent heavier than their mates, nearly identical in plumage but with streaks on the breast. —NICK DUNLOP

Aplomado Falcons take over abandoned stick nests of other raptors and ravens. The nests are usually in large yuccas or mesquites. This nest was in the tightly packed center of a yucca, impenetrable to predators like Great Horned Owls and nearly so for the female falcon. She often struggled to climb in and out to attend to the young, pictured here peering out. —NICK DUNLOP

Aplomado Falcons are sprinters, adept at aerial tail chases after birds, skilled in steep dives. They are extremely fast and maneuverable, using their long tails for braking and tight turns. —NICK DUNLOP

Aluminum bands placed on the falcon's legs by the Peregrine Fund identify an individual. Several generations of wild Aplomados have bred since reintroduction efforts began in the 1990s in southern Texas. —NICK DUNLOP

The Aplomado Falcon, here landing on a blooming yucca, is a colorful and unmistakable addition to the desert landscape, and a year-round resident. —NICK DUNLOP

Subtle physical traits such as smaller feet, different plumage patterns, and slightly smaller size differentiate the Whiskered Screech-Owl from the Eastern and Western Screech Owls. Voice is the best defining distinction. —ROB PALMER

Whiskered Screech-Owls eat insects and inhabit shady canyons and dense pine and oak forests on mountainsides. Wildfire suppression in the past has permitted foliage to thicken in many areas of the West, benefitting these birds. —ROB PALMER

Harris's Hawk

Permanent residents in arid mesquite country of Arizona, Texas, and New Mexico, Harris's Hawks require water to bathe and drink and will even use a livestock water tank. —ROB PALMER

Also known as the Bay-winged Hawk, the Harris's Hawk is the most social of raptors, a fact discovered during study of the North American subspecies in the 1970s and 1980s. —KATE DAVIS

The complex cooperative hunting strategies of Harris's Hawks have been likened to those of a pack of wolves. Related and unrelated groups of usually five birds work together to chase, ambush, and flush prey, sharing the quarry in order of social rank, although the adults usually allow the juveniles to feed first. —ROB PALMER

Harris's Hawks breed year-round, and may be monogamous, polyandrous (the female mating with more than one male), and occasionally polygynous (the male mating with more than one female). Nesting is a social affair, with as many as seven birds, adults and immatures, sharing in nesting duties. Curiously, this cooperative breeding is restricted to the northern race and is not observed in birds in South America. —ROB PALMER

Juveniles look very different from adults until the first molt.—ROB PALMER

Females can be as much as 47 percent heavier than males and have a more powerful flight. Very popular in the sport of falconry, trained Harris's Hawks have been known to chase rabbits on foot, even underground into their burrows. —ROB PALMER

A Harris's Hawk has killed a squirrel and guards it from thieves with wings and tail outstretched, a behavior called mantling. They typically feed on medium-sized mammals such as cottontails and jackrabbits, and birds such as quail. —KATE DAVIS

Harris's Hawks were named to honor Edward Harris, a friend and patron of John James Audubon. The species name, *unicinctus*, means "once girdled," referring to the white ring around the base of the tail. —KATE DAVIS

Harris's Hawks perch in the open to look for prey. They are known to stand on the back of another where perches are scarce, a behavior called stacking. Three birds were observed once in this totem-pole arrangement for more than five minutes. —KATE DAVIS

A trained Harris's Hawk catches a cottontail. —ROB PALMER

References

BOOKS:

Bent, Arthur Cleveland. 1937. *Life Histories of North American Birds of Prey: California Condor, Vultures, Kites, Hawks, Eagles, American Osprey.* New York: Dover Publications.

Bent, Arthur Cleveland. 1937. *Life Histories of North American Birds of Prey: Falcons, Hawks, Caracaras, Owls.* New York: Dover Publications.

Brown, Leslie, and Dean Amadon. 1989. *Eagles, Hawks, and Falcons of the World.* Secaucus, N.J.: Wellfleet Press.

Cade, Tom J. 1982. *The Falcons of the World.* Ithaca, N.Y.: Comstock Publishing Associates, Cornell University Press.

Campbell, Bruce, and Elizabeth Lack. 1985. *A Dictionary of Birds.* Vermillion, S. Dak.: Buteo Books.

Clark, William S., and Brian K. Wheeler. 1987. *Peterson Field Guide: Hawks.* Boston: Houghton Mifflin.

Davis, Kate. 2008. *Falcons of North America.* Missoula, Mont.: Mountain Press Publishing Company.

Del Hoyo, Josep, Andrew Elliott, and Jordi Sargatal, eds. 1994. *Handbook of the Birds of the World, Volume 2: New World Vultures to Guineafowl.* Barcelona: Lynx Edicions.

Del Hoyo, Josep, Andrew Elliott, Jordi Sargatal, and Nigel Collar, eds. 1999. *Handbook of the Birds of the World, Volume 5: Barn Owls to Hummingbirds.* Barcelona: Lynx Edicions.

Dunne, Pete, David Sibley, and Clay Sutton. 1988. *Hawks in Flight.* Boston: Houghton Mifflin.

Ferguson-Lees, James, and David A. Christie. 2001. *Raptors of the World.* Boston: Houghton Mifflin.

Grossman, Mary Louise, and John Hamlet. 1964. *Birds of Prey of the World.* New York: C. N. Potter.

Johnsgard, Paul A. 1988. *North American Owls: Biology and Natural History.* Washington, D.C.: Smithsonian Institution Press.

Johnsgard, Paul A. 1990. *Hawks, Eagles, and Falcons of North America.* Washington, D.C.: Smithsonian Institution Press.

Lynch, Wayne. 2007. *Owls of the United States and Canada.* Baltimore: Johns Hopkins University Press.

Macdonald, Helen. 2001. *Falcon.* London: Reaktion Books.

Morris, Desmond. 2009. *Owl.* London: Reaktion Books.

National Geographic Society. 1999. *Field Guide to the Birds of North America.* Third Edition. Washington, D.C.: National Geographic.

Newton, Ian. 1979. *Population Ecology of Raptors.* Berkhamsted, England: T. & A. D. Poyser.

Peeters, Hans, 2007. *Field Guide to Owls of California and the West.* Berkeley: University of California Press.

Peeters, Hans, and Pam Peeters. 2005. *Raptors of California.* Berkeley: University of California Press.

Poole, A., and F. Gill, eds. 2000. *The Birds of North America.* Ithaca, N.Y.: Cornell Laboratory of Ornithology and American Ornithologists Union

Sibley, David Allen. 2000. *The Sibley Guide to Birds.* New York: Alfred A. Knopf.

Snyder, Noel, and Helen Snyder. 1991. *Birds of Prey: Natural History and Conservation of North American Raptors.* Minneapolis, Minn.: Voyageur Press.

Wheeler, Brian K. 2007. *Raptors of Western North America.* Princeton, N.J.: Princeton University Press.

Wheeler, Brian K., and William S. Clark. 2003. *A Photographic Guide to North American Raptors.* Princeton, N.J.: Princeton University Press.

WEBSITES:

American Ornithologists' Union
www.aou.org

The Birds of North America Online, Cornell Lab of Ornithology
http://bna.birds.cornell.edu/bna

Species Index

Peregrine Falcon. —KATE DAVIS